The Great
Apparitions
of Mary

The Great Apparitions of Mary

An Examination of
Twenty-two Supranormal Appearances

INGO SWANN

A Crossroad Book
The Crossroad Publishing Company
New York

1996

The Crossroad Publishing Company
370 Lexington Avenue, New York, NY 10017

Copyright © 1996 by Ingo Swann

Printed in the United States of America

Library of Congress Cataloging-in-Publication Data

Swann, Ingo, 1933-
    The great apparitions of Mary : an examination of the twenty-two supranormal appearances / Ingo Swann.
        p. cm.
    ISBN 0-8245-1614-1 (pbk.)
    1. Mary, Blessed Virgin, Saint – Apparitions and Miracles – History.
    2. Parapsychology – Religious aspects – Christianity.   I. Title.
    BT650.S92   1996
    232.91 – dc20   96-20510
                                                                       CIP

Contents

Acknowledgments   7

Introduction   9

1. Guadalupe, Mexico (1531)   21

2. Paris, France (1830)   39

3. La Salette, France (1846)   54

4. Lourdes, France (1858)   69

5. Pontmain, France (1871)   85

6. Knock, Ireland (1879)   96

7. Tilly-sur-Seulles, France (1896)   106

8. Mantara, Lebanon (1908, 1911)   113

9. Fátima, Portugal (1917)   119

10. Beauraing, Belgium (1932, 1933)   134

11. Banneux, Belgium (1933)   144

12. Kerizinen, France (1938)   149

13. Lipa, Philippines (1948, 1949)   161

14. Necedah, Wisconsin (1949)   165

15. Jerusalem, Israel (1954)   177

16. Garabandal, Spain (1961) — 182

17. San Damiano, Italy (1964) — 191

18. Montichiari, Italy (1947, 1966) — 198

19. Zeitoun, Egypt (1968) — 205

20. Bayside, Queens, New York (1970) — 211

21. Medjugorje, Yugoslavia (1981) — 219

22. Kibeho, Rwanda (1981) — 226

Epilogue — 235

Bibliography — 237

Acknowledgments

My in-depth research of the Marian apparitions began in 1978, and I'm exceedingly grateful for those many who aided in what turned out to be a difficult task involving over three hundred sources. I am especially grateful to the good offices of the Catholic archdiocese of New York, which during 1984 and 1985 helped me understand the theological evolution regarding the position of Mary. I'm indebted to the Religious News Service for helping obtain obscure news clippings; to the New York Public Library; to the cooperative staff of the Canadian publication *Michael;* to *The Fatima Crusader;* to *Ave Maria,* published in England; and to those who contributed information regarding the apparitions in the United States.

I wish to thank the following individuals: M. M. Castillo, for help in translating parts of Portuguese and Spanish documents; Martin Ebon for help in German translation; Mauricette Durant for overseeing my translation of the French pamphlet regarding the apparition at Kibeho, Rwanda; Reverend James Nichols, a frequent visitor to the apparitional site at Medjugorje, Yugoslavia; the late Marjorie A. N. Cooper-Smith, who helped discover information about the little-known apparitions in Lebanon and Jerusalem; and Jean-Luc Rivera, who helped obtain rare documents in France.

I owe a special debt of gratitude to Cyril Marystone, a devout lay Mariologist who tried to ensure that I write nothing offensive to the Marian faithful; the late Episcopalian Mariologist Reverend Michael Koonsman; and especially the Protestant Mariologist Reverend Paul Lambourne Higgins.

I've had much excellent advice and guidance from many, and I'm thankful for all of it. In the end, though, I've had to strike a particular new path regarding this overview of the apparitions which attempts to focus exclusively on their amazing phenomena. Any errors of commission, omission, misinterpretation, or misunderstanding are my own.

Introduction

In our postmodern times, the term "apparition" is not as magnetic and universally known as it has been throughout most of human history. There are a number of reasons for this. An apparition is a paranormal event. Mainstream science rejected the paranormal during the first half of the twentieth century by distinguishing between the rational and the irrational. The irrational was not a proper topic for scientific study. So the study of the paranormal lacked support not only in the sciences, but within scholarship and academe.

Very few people really ever saw an apparition. So it was easy enough to insulate the rational logic of science from this tiny, irrational minority by casting the minority into the "lunatic fringe." Seers of apparitions could then be considered as victims of hallucinations, or as mentally unsound, when compared to what was considered psychologically and scientifically normal.

During the second half of this century, though, the mind was discovered to possess different levels of consciousness and different "dimensions." Researchers began to be less sure regarding what constituted mental "normality," and so concepts regarding the mind began to change. At first the changes occurred only in psychology. But then physics, formerly focused only on the constituents of physical matter, became involved and began to change too.

It was seen in physics that mind, at some of its levels, interacted with matter in ways that could not be accounted for by strict physical cause-and-effect. Albeit very slowly, it was eventually concluded that a nonmaterial kind of physics existed, which involved phenomena with which the human mind interacted.

So the "problems" of mind and consciousness began to be seen as "interactive" with the "problems" of physics, which now included both material and nonmaterial phenomena. Past concepts of matter, energy, space and time, once undoubted, began to undergo modification and change and to be redefined not by psychologists but by physicists. By the 1980s, it was concluded that space and time consisted of different dimensions within which matter and energy behaved differently.

Reassessments of phenomena experienced in the past but rejected by most now began to take place. Major among these were the so-called "near-death experiences" (NDEs), which had been recorded since time immemorial. A person clinically dead comes back to life and reports traveling while "dead" to various transcendental dimensions or realms. The sheer bulk of near-death experience reports aroused the profound need to redefine concepts of psychology itself.

In early 1994, the influential American Psychiatric Association (APA) extracted near-death-experiences from the category of "bizarre delusions" — the psychological category or "trash bin" into which all paranormal phenomena had been consigned.

To the shock of the entire Western world, the APA did an about-face regarding near-death experiences. In its *Diagnostic and Statistical Manual of Mental Disorders* the APA now suggested, albeit with caution, the positive consideration by therapists of NDEs and certain other paranormal experiences.

Important to the subject of this book is that those experiencing a near-death event reported encountering not only family and friends who had passed over, but orbs of intelligent light, guides, guardians, angels, religious figures, and even the Savior Himself. These near-death experiences, then, at least verged on the realms or dimensions traditionally recognized as holy.

Among the most exceptional of exceptional experiences are the great apparitions of the Holy Mother, Mary, Queen of Heaven, Mother of Humanity. Certain elements are relevant to all of the major apparitions of the Holy Mother and help constitute the larger backdrop within which the events occur.

The Confusion of Sources

The first may be called "the confusion of sources." No problems may be apparent if you read one source regarding a given apparition. But if you read five or ten regarding the same apparition, then many of the reputed facts don't altogether correspond.

Simply put, different authors write about the apparitions in different ways thus producing different versions, and ultimately one has to become a kind of sleuth to sort through the various versions of "the facts." I've decided to depend mostly upon the earliest sources available to me.

The Extraordinary Phenomena

The extraordinary phenomena consist of what the seers and witnesses say they saw, predictions made by the Lady which were fulfilled, the Lady's messages, and the miraculous cures.

The messages and the cures constitute an enormous amount of material. I've selected from among the messages only those which can be shown as timely and germane to earthly events. Regarding the very many claimed cures, I've selected only those few which played an important part regarding the unfolding of the apparitional events themselves.

There are two kinds of the great apparitions, referred to as "speaking" and "nonspeaking." In some of the speaking apparitions, the Lady's messages can be quite stern, and such messages are often deleted or weakened in the accounts of the apparitions, especially if embarrassing to church authorities. I've included such messages where it seems appropriate.

The Human Actors

An apparition of the Holy Mother is always a complex affair which unfolds as "sequences." The human side of the affair may involve thousands of people, and even many millions. The human side consists of a cast of at least seven sets of people.

- The *seers* of the Lady herself are relatively few in number. In all cases, the seers have been children or educationally challenged adults.

- The *witnesses* are those among the pilgrims or others who have arrived who themselves claim also to see the appearing Lady, or if not her, then some of the magnificent and astonishing phenomena. The witnesses play an important role in all of the major apparitions.

- From their onset, all of the great Marian apparitions have quickly (often overnight) attracted large, sometimes massive, groups of *devout pilgrims* as well as the curious. These play distinct roles in the unfolding of the events.

- The *ecclesiastics*, representing the church, at first are often ill disposed to the apparitions, often work to discredit them, and try to ignore them. Even so, the ecclesiastics ultimately have to make decisions regarding the apparition's authenticity.

- Most of the apparitions occur in small hamlets or out-of-the way places. The *civil authorities* at first feel it their duty to interrogate the seers. But since the massive influx of pilgrims to the apparitional site can very quickly grow to fifty thousand or more, in a short time the civil authorities become preoccupied solely with mob and traffic control and sanitation matters.

- All of the modern apparitions (1830–present) have quickly attracted some kind of *media* interest, which is sometimes extensive.

- The *skeptics* are also attracted. Their purpose is to debunk "the evidence," in some instances patently trying to make a name for themselves.

The interactions between these seven groups contribute to the social dramatics, confusion, and pandemonium.

The accompanying table lists the great apparitions considered in this book. The emphasis is on "Seers/Witnesses."

Date or Beginning Date	Place	Seers/witnesses
1531, December	Mexico	1 seer, 6(?) witnesses
1830, July	Paris, France	1 seer
1846, September	La Salette, France	2 seers, many witnesses
1858, February	Lourdes, France	1 seer, many witnesses
1871, January	Pontmain, France	4–6 seers
1879, August	Knock, Ireland	200+ witnesses
1896, March	Tilly-sur-Seulles, France	400+ witnesses and experiencers
1911, June	Mantara, Lebanon	200+ witnesses
1917, May	Fátima, Portugal	3 seers, 70,000+ witnesses
1932, November	Beauraing, Belgium	5 seers, witnesses
1933, January	Banneux, Belgium	1 seer, witnesses
1938, September	Kerizinen, France	1 seer, hundreds of witnesses
1948, September	Lipa, Philippines	1 seer, thousands of witnesses
1949, November	Necedah, Wisconsin	1 seer, witnesses
1954, July	Jerusalem, Israel	200+ witnesses
1961, June	Garabandal, Spain	4 seers, 1,000+ witnesses
1964, October	San Damiano, Italy	1 seer, 10,000+ witnesses, first alleged photo
1966, February	Montichiari, Italy	1 seer, thousands of witnesses
1968, April	Zeitoun, Egypt	500,000+ witnesses, unchallenged photos
1970, June	Bayside, New York	1 seer, 1,000+ witnesses
1981, June	Medjugorje, Yugoslavia	5 seers, hundreds of witnesses
1981, November	Kibeho, Rwanda	7–9 principal seers, numerous witnesses

Religious Treatment of the Apparitions

Catholic theologians have always agreed that God can grant private revelations, suspending the normal laws which veil from mortals the persons and realities of the supernatural world and manifesting them to direct sensory or intellectual perception of selected individuals. Both the Old and the New Testaments record such occurrences, and it would be rash to eliminate on an a priori basis the possibility of contemporary revelations.

There may be an apparition or a vision, corporeal or imaginative, of Jesus Christ, of His Blessed Mother, or of angels or saints. The central concern, however, is whether an apparition is of divine or diabolical origin.

Article 1399 of the Canon Law forbade the publication of certain books such as those that dealt with revelations, visions, prophecies, miracles, and apparitions. Article 2318 carried penalties against those who violated the laws of censure and prohibition. The concept of ecclesiastical approval or disapproval of apparitions emanated from the treatise *De servorum Dei beatificationis* issued by Pope Benedict XIV, who reigned from 1740 to 1758. The treatise established that the Roman Catholic Church might give approval of an apparition only after careful investigation. This approval allowed for only the assent of human faith; it did not require the assent of Catholic faith. Competence for this decision-making rested with the bishop of the diocese within which the apparition occurred.

In 1966, however, when three of the great apparitions included in this book were ongoing, a decree of the Sacred Congregation for the Doctrine and the Faith was published, dated December 29, 1966. The decree had been approved on October 14, 1966, by Pope Paul VI, who ordered its publication.

The decree abrogated all previous stipulations regarding apparitions. Ecclesiastical permission was no longer required for the publication of information about apparitions, revelations, visions, or miracles. Since then, none can incur ecclesiastical censure for frequenting places of apparitions, even those not recognized by the ordinaries of dioceses or by the Holy Father.

The Secular Context

Because the religious and secular worlds are considered to be separate, secular interest in the apparitions of the Holy Mother has generally been avoided, and reports of apparitions have been suppressed in academe and the secular media. Most people have thus learned very little or nothing at all about the great apparitions.

Many accounts of the apparitions tend to lift them out of the contemporary social contexts within which they occurred, sometimes ignoring the messages of the Lady aimed at those particular contexts. Yet some of the great apparitions have had tremendous consequences for their social contexts. The full impact of an apparition of the Holy Mother cannot be appreciated unless it is considered in its social context. I have therefore made an effort to summarize those contexts.

The Witnesses and the "Grassroots" Devout

In most documents regarding the holy apparitions, the historical treatment of the witnesses is perplexing. On the one hand thousands of people have been eyewitnesses to incredible phenomena taking place at the sites of the apparitions. On the other hand, their testimony has consistently been minimized and considered as infectious hysteria or mass hallucination. Yet a great deal of direct eyewitness testimony regarding the holy apparitions is remarkably consistent.

The great apparitions of the Holy Mother are made so by the responses of what I'll call (with no disrespect intended) the grassroots devout. Typically the secular and religious authorities at first have no intention of permitting an apparition to be "authenticated" as of divine or holy origin. The Holy Mother seems to speak in some kind of a collective way to the hearts of the grassroots devout, after which the devout will go to extraordinary lengths to visit the site of the Lady's appearances. Thus thousands of witnesses may be present to observe the major miracles at close hand.

If the devout are responding to Mary's call, then there is nothing church, science, or philosophy can do about it. Such is the power of Mary's apparitions to the devout, and her power seems to be theirs and theirs alone. Through the years I've developed an abiding respect, not only for the intentions of the lay and religious devout, but also for their collective power.

The Terms

Certain terms are important in any consideration of the apparitions. We use the terms today, but have largely departed from their earlier and more powerful meanings.

The standard definition of "apparition" is an unusual or unexpected sight or phenomenon, usually described as a ghostly figure or appearance. This has led modern people to think of a ghost as an apparition. In the past, though, a ghost was referred to as a phantom or specter or an appearing soul in order to distinguish it from an apparition of a saint, angel, Jesus, or the Holy Mother.

In parallel with "apparition," one of the definitions of "appearance" refers to an outward aspect, an external show, something that paranormally appears externally.

As we will see, these two terms — "apparition" and "appearance" — are not always adequate to the task at hand in this book. But they are the best ones we have, and so we will use them.

There is a perpetual confusion between a "vision" and an "apparition," and the two terms are often used interchangeably. A "vision," however, is most often experienced internally, as if in "one's head." Many have experienced visions of the Virgin. But an apparition is always experienced as external, and at a well-defined point, place, or space outside of one's body and mind. If, for example, multiple seers are involved, they will all look at the same spot regardless of how they are physically arranged. In some cases, witnesses of apparitional phenomena have been distributed around a twenty-mile-wide circle. All of them have looked toward the center of the circle, where they saw independently confirmed phenomena.

The existence of holy realms was rejected by modern mainstream philosophy and science as superstition, bunk, and illusion. This rejection in fact separated religion from science, to the relief of both sides.

The term "holy" is taken from an Old European word referring to the supernatural. We have to remind ourselves that in most premodern societies the supernatural did not refer to illusions or delusions, as has been taught during the modern period. Rather, "supernatural" referred to invisible realms of forces and powers which existed "above" the visible, natural realms. These invisible realms were holy ones, and their existence was generally unquestioned.

Physics today is finding that realms "above" the natural do exist. Most modern peoples, though, do not accept the existence of the invisible realms.

There once was a nuance to the term "holy" which is now seldom acknowledged. The holy was something awesome, ominous, frightening, and filled with superhuman and potentially fatal power. This former meaning is still given in dictionaries, although considered obsolete.

This nuance is very important to our consideration of the apparitions of the Holy Mother. She and the amazing phenomena which accompany her are exquisite, beautiful, and wonderful. She comes, however, not as a messenger of sweetness and light, but as an admonisher with ominous warnings.

"Apocalypse" refers to an imminent cosmic cataclysm through which God destroys the ruling powers of evil and their human minions. The apocalyptic content of the Lady's messages does not sit very well with either religious or secular authorities. Thus this content is usually avoided, sometimes deleted from sources, while apparitions which dwell at length on this subject are seldom seen as authentic.

Our English word "miracle" is taken from the Latin *mirari*, which meant "to wonder at." But the Latin term was taken from the far more ancient Sanskrit term *smayate*, meaning "he smiles." The modern English meaning of "miracle" is "an extraordinary event manifesting a supernatural work of God." A miracle occurs when God smiles, an action which really can't be translated into either English or logic.

Indeed, for a miracle to be considered as such, it has to defy logic and common sense, and the laws of matter, energy, space, and time as well. There is no such thing as a mundane or an explainable miracle, because if one could be explained then it would not be supernatural — not one of God's smiles.

There is a link between the meanings of "holy" and "sacred," which meant set apart for worship of a deity or entitled to reverence. We still define "sacred" in this sense today, but have removed it from the meaning of "holy" as a separate realm.

In her great speaking apparitions, the Lady's words quite clearly are utilizing the former rather than the modern meanings of such words. If this is not understood, then many of the Lady's messages cannot be comprehended.

But if these older meanings are understood, then it becomes clear, for example, that the appearing Lady considers humanity as sacred and holy and that she often condemns the loss of this sense among us. In premodern times, it was generally understood that the holy and the sacred should be considered with some seriousness. This is abundantly clear in the messages.

If an appearance of the Holy Mother took place only in our heads, as in a vision, then it could be compared to a dream, whether of one awake or asleep. Dream experiences can be very real and can incorporate the dreamer into the dream. But we do not expect that anything dreamed is tangible, having some kind of external presence in the ways that objective, physical realities do.

The major apparitions of the Holy Mother, though, are external events, external to those who see them and to the witnesses of their astonishing phenomena. As we define the differences between tangible and intangible, the apparitions are intangible, yet external and located at a given place and perceived as if they were tangible.

In some cases the Lady is seen as completely physical with a physical presence exactly like any other human being. Far more frequently, however, she is seen as floating in the air and transparent. But her "physical" presence is still abundantly sensed, and the astonishing phenomena which accompany her are seen and felt to be tangible, but are not.

Among the elements of an apparition which correspond to our definition of "tangible" are the miraculous cures which obviously involve human anatomy. Healing springs which well up are also tangible, and the Lady left a very tangible artefact during her apparitions in Mexico in 1531.

The distinctions between "tangible" and "intangible" are quite inadequate when it comes to an apparition of the Holy Mother. Skeptics have always insisted that the intangible does not exist. If something was seen but was intangible, then it was judged as a figment of the mind.

Anything that can be photographed, however, is accepted as being tangible enough; many skeptics have held that until an apparition is photographed there is no reason to accept it.

The Hologram Metaphor

In human terms, anything that is inexplicable has to be compared to something that is explicable and aids in giving some kind of understanding regarding the inexplicable. It is the function of the "metaphor" to suggest a likeness or analogy between what can be explained and what cannot.

Prior to the 1960s, no metaphor existed which could be applied to the apparitions of the Holy Mother. She literally appeared where there was nothing. She and the phenomena accompanying her were seen by her seers and witnesses. If this was the case, then the physical mechanisms of the eyes were involved. The question then was: how could something which was not there be there in a way that registered on the mechanisms of the eye?

During the 1960s, however, the techniques of holography were invented — and for the first time a useful metaphor was available. Technically speaking, holograms are formed by projections of coherent light so that they form interference patterns where the light intersects. Three-dimensional images are reproduced at a designated interference place. Images can be projected this way into an empty space.

Holographic images formed this way appear completely external. They also appear to be three-dimensional, having bulk, shape, and mass. They are apparently tangible — until one sticks a finger through them. If motion picture film or computer equipment is utilized, the image will even make motions in a completely empty space.

Thus, through holographic techniques, something can appear where nothing really is, something which can clearly be seen by the unaided human eye. And the hologram images can be photographed exactly as if they were really there. The hologram is intangible by our usual definition of that word, yet it can be photographed as if it were completely tangible. The hologram metaphor, however, cannot totally explain all or any of the apparitions of the Holy Mother.

The first completely unchallengeable photographs of an apparition of the Holy Mother were taken in 1968. The apparition at

Zeitoun, Egypt, was captured on film by thousands of cameras. One principal criterion of the skeptics was thus fulfilled.

This much-photographed event thus made it mandatory — at least among those interested — to begin reassessing the claims of past witnesses of other apparitions and of the seers themselves. And it is this reassessment which is the principal purpose of this book.

1

Guadalupe, Mexico

(1531)

The mighty drama of the conquest of Mexico began in 1519, eighteen years after Columbus on behalf of Spain first reached the shores of those jewel-like islands afterward called the Bahamas. Spain was the most powerful nation of Europe at the time, and immediately after Columbus's arrival the Spanish quickly undertook the dramatic necessities of making the New World theirs.

Not only were discovery and territory involved, but also one other exciting factor that always inspires men to undertake extreme activity — gold!

As it turned out, though, gold was not in abundance on any of the islands. The conquered island natives pointed to the west, to the Great Land Kingdoms across the Caribbean Sea. There, they said, the rulers had gold in the abundance the Spanish sought.

So in 1511, the first Spanish governor of Cuba, Diego de Velázquez, turned his eyes to the west, as did every one else. There ensued seven years of political intrigues concerning who would lead the first expedition to Mexico.

Finally, in 1518 the governor selected Hernán Cortés and signed a contract with him which would ensure Cortés's rights in perpetuity as captain-general of Mexico. The contract was in due course approved in the name of the Spanish king, Charles I, by the powerful Jeronymite Fathers, who had established their headquarters in Santo Domingo. The fathers' great and important preoccupation was the religious conversion of the conquered native inhabitants of the New World.

The contract outraged Cortés's contenders, for it awarded him not only unparalleled eminence, but governance of all Mexico. Probably more to the point, it also awarded him personally at least one-sixth of all the wealth of the great Aztec empire once conquered.

So intrigues were set afoot to bribe Velázquez to revoke the appointment, and Cortés was soon warned that it would be. He, however, had already spent all he had, extensively borrowed on credit, and had enlisted some three hundred men for the expedition. A bit short on supplies, he outfoxed his enemies by sailing his troops and ships secretly in the dead of night. He arrived early in 1519 in the environs of the hot, humid Yucatan Peninsula. Cortés was thirty-three at the time.

Now commenced one of the greatest cultural conflicts of all time, one of renown or infamy — depending on how we look at it through our own contemporary lenses.

Cortés had a series of misadventures along the Yucatan coast, but his three hundred troops prevailed against opposition which sometimes numbered twenty thousand native inhabitants. It was realized that the Yucatan was not just another island but part of a large land mass, which Cortés named New Spain. After winning battles with the Indians at the Tabasco River, he headed toward the northwest, to "Mexico."

Sailing up along the coast, he arrived in the tropical area of Veracruz, where a long, drawn-out negotiation commenced to approach the Aztec emperor, Moctezuma II, who dwelled in the distant highlands in the fabled city of Tenochtitlán. Meanwhile, Cortés forged an alliance with the powerful Tlascalans, who wished to escape the domination of the Aztec emperor.

The stay at Veracruz was demoralizing, for the Spanish found much objectionable among the natives, while the Indians were astonished at the Spanish.

For one thing, the hot, humid environs of Veracruz were hell to the Spanish. The Indians went about nearly naked and bathed several times a day. The Spanish considered bathing unmanly and so never did it. They were horrified by the nudity, and the Indians recoiled from the stink of Cortés's men. There was also confusion regarding organized sexual practices of the Indians. These details, however, were amenable to compromise and were surmounted.

But never to be reconciled were the patterns of human sacrifice and ritual cannibalism practiced upon enemies, with the chief sacrificial center of the Aztec empire being at Tenochtitlán. The Indians didn't understand this Spanish objection completely, largely because Cortés had some of his rebellious men burned at the stake. The Indians were astonished because the white men roasted each other, but wasted the cooked flesh by not eating it afterward.

So these were stressful times for the Spanish, and soon faced with a full mutiny, Cortés deliberately sank all his boats — thereby committing the Spanish irrevocably to taking Mexico.

Messages received from Moctezuma II showed he was delaying permission for Cortés to proceed to Tenochtitlán. So, taking the initiative, Cortés now set out across the central mountains into the highlands, determined to seize Tenochtitlán. There he and his men arrived in November 1519 after some fighting along the way with natives.

The beautiful and exceedingly elegant city of Tenochtitlán was at a fresh and cool elevation of seven thousand feet in a vast valley. It was surrounded by the blue waters of the grand Lake Texcoco. As modern reconstructions of it show, Tenochtitlán was one of the all-time great wonders of the world, its extensive buildings and temples gleaming and colorful.

But among these temples were two great pyramids rising high above all. Atop these took place ritual human sacrifice, which enabled Moctezuma II to psychically commune with the Aztec gods to learn their wishes and instructions.

The Spanish, their lips clenched at the sight of these two monuments, were nonetheless at first received well by Moctezuma II, largely it is said because some of his advisors believed that the white men in their gleaming armor and astride horses were the white gods of their legends.

Hostilities soon arose between the Aztecs and the aggressive white men searching for and demanding gold and other commodities. The Aztec patience became shorter. Some of Cortés's men, outnumbered by several thousand to one, managed to commit some atrocities, for which they were seized and sacrificed — after which things went from bad to worse.

In retaliation, the Aztec emperor was then seized as hostage, which outraged all in the Aztec empire. The Spanish didn't fully realize that the person of Moctezuma II, as highest of the priests, was sacred and that his imprisonment meant that the Aztec gods now disapproved of him. The emperor could no longer maintain control and the Aztec society began coming apart.

Moctezuma II was inadvertently killed when one of his own people threw a rock which struck his head. More white men were captured and sacrificed. Soon the Spanish had to retreat, fighting their way out of the city with heavy losses in the bloody confusion of the *Noche triste* (Sad Night) of July 1, 1520.

After winning other battles in the surrounding area, a year later Cortés returned to Tenochtitlán, captured the city, and destroyed the power of the Aztec nobility. The Aztec peoples, however, numbering many millions, were entirely another matter.

Although Cortés extended his conquest by sending out his lieutenants over Mexico and Central America, new Spanish troops, political forces, and priests flooded into Mexico and to Tenochtitlán. Cortés's power was challenged, and he temporarily returned to Spain (1528–30) to petition the king.

Although he was treated cordially by the Spanish king, who had now become Holy Roman Emperor Charles V, his absolute powers were taken from him and given to the Spanish viceroy, Antonio de Mendoza.

Before Cortés was dethroned, so to speak, one of his first acts at Tenochtitlán was to demolish the great pyramids. A cathedral was to be erected on the site of Moctezuma's chief sacrificial temple.

Ultimately, the wondrous city of Tenochtitlán was leveled, thence to be called Mexico City.

Throughout the Aztec empire, however, were many other similar temples, at which some twenty thousand human sacrifices were made annually. Missionaries soon arrived in Mexico City and attempted to open churches, schools, and hospitals and to convert the natives. But the deep-rooted Aztec traditions proved hard to eradicate. Conversions were relatively few, and sacrifices continued elsewhere.

Because of this, and also because of various Spanish cruelties and abuses of the natives, the new country now proved troublesome to control. Charles V sent an emissary who found it virtually impossible to cope with the volatile situation. So the emissary was replaced in 1528 by five administrators, later known as the First *Audiencia,* or "Audience"; a Second Audience was soon necessary to replace the first one.

The administrative duties of the First Audience, headed by Don Nuño de Guzmán, were secular in nature, to establish and enforce civil law. Charles V gave extraordinary and inquisitorial powers to Guzmán and the First Audience.

But it is certain that Guzmán and his administrative clique were quite mean men burdened with a variety of dismal attitudes and a not inconsiderable amount of stupidity. For example, Guzmán launched abuses and cruelties upon the Indians — such as rape, torture, and slavery. He justified these atrocities on the grounds that the Aztecs had no souls in the sense Christians did, that they were akin to the monsters of ancient legends. They were subhuman, and they could not therefore be converted.

However, the Spanish population of Mexico was yet quite small, while the Indian population numbered many millions. The Aztecs were known as a fierce and proud people. It was clear to some of the Spanish that the megalomaniac idiocies of Guzmán and the First Audience would lead to trouble.

Back in Spain, the king, when he understood the situation, found it necessary to counterbalance the authority of the First Audience simply to protect the Mexican population from its increasing abuses.

After careful deliberation, Charles V decided to appoint a bishop to Mexico and to arm him with considerable powers. For this task he selected Prior Juan Zumárraga of the Franciscan monastery at Abrojo in Spain, appointing him, in December 1528, as the first bishop of the New World and as the official Protector of the Indians.

Zumárraga was in many ways a remarkable man. Upon his arrival in Mexico City, this new bishop set tirelessly to work for the social welfare of Mexico and for the conversion of the Indians. He prevailed on the church in Spain to send many more missionaries and set up schools to train a native clergy. Among the first of these was one established at Tlaltelolco just north of Mexico City, where a few conversions were made.

Bishop Zumárraga brought with him many excellent economic and civilizing concepts, all of which he tirelessly set into action. But he found it rather hard going when it came to conversions: first because the natives resisted giving up their "Aztec souls" and refused to abandon the ancestral worship of their idols, and second because the First Audience was dominated by Guzmán, who was equally tirelessly exhibiting cruelty and tyranny in the exercise of the powers given him by the same king.

In spite of his other excellent qualities, the new bishop now made at least two mistakes. The first was his prompt excommunication of Guzmán in 1529. However, the excommunication did not deprive Guzmán of the civil powers given to him by the Spanish king.

The result of the excommunication, among other troubles, was that the Guzmán clique instituted censorship on all messages to Spain, soon began assaulting friars, and threatened to prosecute Zumárraga himself.

Early in 1530, Zumárraga managed to get to the Spanish king a message hidden in a crucifix. The king immediately took steps to replace Guzmán and his tyrannical officials with a Second Audience. The Second Audience was headed by Don Sebastián Ramírez y Fuenleal, who was to become the new governor of

Mexico. The new appointments were made in late 1530, but it took about a year for the new appointees to arrive in Mexico City and unseat the Guzmán clique.

Meanwhile, the First Audience increased the torture and murder of Aztec men and women and of their Spanish sympathizers as well, for many Spanish men had begun intermarrying with Aztec women, especially with those of noble lineage and claims to vast tracts of land and wealth. Guzmán justified the cruelty by pointing up that human sacrifice was still going on.

Zumárraga had no defense against this charge — and now made his second great mistake by ordering the destruction of shrines, manuscripts, idols, and relics venerated by the Aztecs. If Guzmán's torture and murder had not been enough of a deterrent to the conversion of the Indians, Zumárraga's culture-destroying tactics now added to that deterrent. And both tactics contributed further to Aztec anger.

The Aztecs and other tribes, many millions strong, began taking up arms against the Spanish. It was clear that a massive and bloody insurrection was boiling up. This portended the annihilation of the relatively few Spanish in Mexico and all of those few Aztecs so far converted. Historians like to say that the Spanish had superior power. But in fact they did not.

Even as the new Second Audience arrived at Mexico City in late 1531, the Guzmán clique did not give up immediately. So it seems unlikely that Ramírez y Fuenleal had time to prevent the retaliation of the Aztecs — especially since the Aztecs, having learned something from the Spanish about fighting, were already gathered and rising up in remote locations.

Such was the ominous crisis on the cold winter day of December 9, 1531. Zumárraga, worried to distraction, was told that an Aztec peasant had requested to see him. Zumárraga was exceedingly busy and kept the peasant waiting for several hours. Finally, since the man hadn't given up and gone away, the bishop recruited an interpreter and had the fellow brought in.

This man carried news which would unfold during the next seven days and which by the end of that month would see the immediate conversion of hundreds of thousands of the Aztecs and the permanent cessation of ritual human sacrifice.

Kneeling down, the peasant, who was fifty-seven at the time, at first didn't know what to say to the august bishop. But the interpreter, most probably a priest named Juan González, encouraged him to speak. So the peasant identified himself as Cuauhtlatohuac ("Singing Eagle"), born into the Aztec servant class, but a Christian convert who had taken the name of Juan Diego.

Frequently, Juan said, he would walk the fifteen miles from his village of Cuautitlán to Tlaltelolco, just north of Mexico City, where he attended early Mass and received the sacraments. But on this very day as he had passed around a familiar hill called Tepeyac he had heard music atop the hill resembling the singing of various birds. Climbing up the 130 feet to the summit, he found a beautiful Lady among the mesquite bushes, prickly pears, and other desert scrubs growing there.

The Lady spoke to him in his own Aztec language, Nahuatl. She asked where he was going, and she then identified herself as the perfect and perpetual Virgin Mary. She desired that a *teocalli* (temple) be built at Tepeyac, where she would hear the weepings and sorrows of all, and where she would remedy sufferings, deprivations, and misfortunes.

She advised that she was the merciful mother of all united in this land, of all inhabitants on this earth, of all those who love her. Go, she said, to the house of the bishop and say that I have sent you. Tell him what you have seen and heard.

The result of the interview with the bishop was that Juan Diego was quickly shown the door.

Juan Diego returned to the Tepeyac hill, where he again found the Lady waiting. He reported the rebuff to her and apparently begged that she select another person of higher standing. She now said that it was only through Juan Diego that the mission could be undertaken, and Juan agreed to try again the next day.

In this ignominious way, and on the edge of the brewing crisis, began an apparitional event which was to have enormous impact throughout the Americas and the world down until today.

It is surprising to find, however, that the reputation and authenticity of this apparition did not rest upon investigations and inquiry to which apparitions are usually submitted.

Rather there is an almost complete absence of records from the 1531 period, allowing skeptics to condemn the apparition as myth and fake contrivances. So it is a full part of the story to understand how and when the apparition finally was accepted as a factual holy event.

The absence of contemporary documents and records of subsequent investigations remains an unsolved mystery. Surely they once existed — and there are some small clues indicating that they did exist. However, only two anywhere near contemporary narrations of the apparitional events in 1531 have been found.

The first is a document which is undated. Because of its particular style of handwriting, exacting modern scholarship has determined that it can have been written only between 1551 and 1561. Since both Juan Diego and Zumárraga died in 1548, the account is obviously some kind of second-hand reconstruction — but with the probability that the author personally knew Juan Diego and/or Zumárraga.

The document is in the Nahuatl language and is called the *Nican Mopohua* (Nahuatl for "an account"), written and signed by an Indian named Antonio Valeriano. It is not a very long account considering the dramatic events it represents.

The document shows some signs of being embellished, especially regarding devotional language and metaphor, and it gives no details of what the Lady looked like. All of the subsequent descriptions of the appearance are based on this single, short narration — and, rather inventively, many go far beyond what it contains. The devout accepted this document as an authentic account, but many skeptics considered it a fake because the existence of Antonio Valeriano could not be confirmed.

And there the matter rather mysteriously rested for well over three hundred years. And were it not for the fact that this apparition produced an amazing physical artifact, which even modern science and technology cannot explain, the whole story might have disappeared in the same mysterious way as its documentation did.

The next thing that is known about the documentation is that in 1558, twenty-seven years after the apparition, a large collection was made of documents in the Nahuatl language referring to it. It might therefore be surmised that official Spanish documents also once existed, but no trace of them has been found. The Nahuatl collection disappeared somewhere along the way, and its existence is known only by a brief mention of it in the famous Boturini Collection.

Scholars thus suspect that both the Nahuatl collection and the contemporary Spanish records might exist in some large library, and many suspect the voluminous Vatican archives or ecclesiastical archives in Spain.

There, again, the matter rested — until the third decade of the twentieth century. It was only in 1924 that anything was discovered resembling a contemporary mention of the apparition to Juan Diego. And then it was found not in Mexico or Spain, but in Tetlapalco, Peru, by the anthropologist H. M. Saville — and is accordingly named after him as the Codex Saville-Tetlapalco.

This document is extremely important since it is now assumed to be the oldest extant book of the Americas; it is housed in the Museum of the American Indian in New York City.

But the codex is not exactly a book. Rather it is an Aztec pictorial symbol calendar that records Aztec history from the year 1430 to 1557. It can be deciphered only by specialists, the first of whom was Mariano Cuevas, who translated it in 1929.

Discs on the calendar were used by the Indians to signify the passage of time, and Cuevas comments as follows regarding a female figure located next to the top of the disc representing the year 1531:

*A virgin with her hands folded near her heart, her head bent
toward the right, in a salmon-colored tunic and a greenish
blue mantilla. This would appear to be the Virgin venerated
at Tepeyac, four miles north of Mexico City. By painting the
disk and figure a little lower than the year 1532, it is well
indicated that her year was 1531.*

The date 1531 is well established in the codex, nor is there
any problem regarding the year the first small chapel was built
at Tepeyac. For its existence shortly after 1532 is mentioned in
several preserved wills bequeathing money and asking for Masses
to be said there. And this chapel, as the "myth" insists, came into
existence because of Juan Diego.

The next piece of documentary evidence of the apparition was
found only in the early 1950s by the Nahuatl scholar Angel M.
Garibay-Kintana, who discovered it in a document in the Mexican National Library Archives. He named the document *The
Primitive Relation*.

This document consists of thirty-nine very brief paragraphs,
which altogether comprise a synopsis of the apparition. Garibay-
Kintana believed it was compiled about 1573 by the historian
Juan de Tovar, who probably transcribed it from earlier sources.

Garibay also believed that one of the earlier sources had been
Juan González, credited by most historians as being one of Zumárraga's translators, who may have interpreted into Spanish
Juan Diego's startling messages in Bishop Zumárraga's palace
in 1531.

The thirty-nine paragraphs, however brief, more or less corre-
late with the "fake" version of Antonio Valeriano found in the
Nican Mopohua.

Recall that the Valeriano version was considered fake only because Valeriano's existence could not be proven. However, during
the 1970s a sixteenth-century civil paper was found in the Mexican National University library bearing the very clear signature of

Antonio Valeriano, which matched the one at the bottom of the *Nican Mopohua*. Antonio Valeriano had been a real person.

The pictograph entered into the Saville Codex calendar for the year 1531 very clearly shows a woman who is not Aztec. The mere entry of this figure into the Aztec calendar shows that it represents an event of momentous importance.

The pictograph and the Valeriano account agree completely on how the Lady was dressed. These two quite independent sources are in accord with the thirty-nine paragraphs in *The Primitive Relation*. Hence, by the 1970s there could be no way of getting around these three unimpeachable discoveries: the apparition to Juan Diego *did happen* in 1531.

The biographical details of Juan Diego are sketchy. He was born in 1474, married but childless, and lived in the village of Cuautitlán some fifteen miles to the north of Tenochtitlán (Mexico City.)

At the time of the apparition, he had only one remaining family member, his uncle Juan Bernardino, who lived in the village of Tolpetlac six miles south of Cuautitlán. Both are described as poor and humble Aztec farmers.

In 1525, the famous Aztec princess Papantzin was among the first to be converted to Christianity, and a small rush of conversions followed, which included Juan Diego, his wife, who took the name of María Lucía, and his uncle, who took the name of Juan Bernardino. María Lucía died shortly thereafter.

Several portraits alleged to be of Juan Diego exist, showing a luxuriantly bearded man. But Juan Diego was Aztec and of beardless genetic stock, and so the portraits are probably inventions. Indeed, the Aztec emperor Moctezuma II was extremely proud of his *three* chin hairs, which caused the full-bearded Spanish to giggle at him.

Juan Diego had four encounters with the apparition, the first of which has already been narrated. When he reported back to the Lady his failure, she ordered him to return again to the bishop's palace, which he did, and was again rebuffed.

But this time Zumárraga demanded that the Lady provide him with a "sign from heaven," which he left up to her to decide upon. Scurrying once more to Tepeyac hill, Juan reported the bishop's request to her; she told him to return the next day and she would provide the sign.

That evening, however, upon his return to his village, he visited his uncle, whom he found stricken either with *cocolixtle,* a dreaded fever that invariably claimed the lives of its many victims, or with a form of plague equally deadly. The village physician tried to help, but the condition worsened, and so Juan did not return to the Tepeyac hill the next day.

By that night it became apparent that the uncle would die, and he begged Juan to hurry to Tlaltelolco to call a priest to hear his confession and administer the last sacraments. Juan set off in the dark cold about four in the morning, walking fast. It was December 12, 1531.

Again he had to pass by the Tepeyac hill. Since he didn't want to be delayed if the Lady was waiting for him he tried to sneak past on the opposite side of the hill. But he was startled to see the Lady descending the hill to intersect with his path. And there she was again, in front of him, smiling and asking what was the matter.

The Lady then advised Juan that his uncle was "cured at this very moment" and that Juan should now climb the hill where he had seen her previously and gather the many flowers he would find there and bring them back down to her.

To his amazement, at the crest of Tepeyac hill he found in the cold winter air a profusion of various kinds of flowers. These were growing from among the rocks, thistles, cactus, and mesquite bushes. He noticed that the flowers glittered with dew drops and exuded delightful fragrances. He tried to gather up all the flowers, but there were a great many of them.

To have something to carry the flowers he took off his *tilma* — soon to become one of the most famous pieces of clothing in history. A *tilma* is a traditional Aztec long-cloak or cape worn around the body and tied at the neck; it is commonly made in two pieces with a seam at the back. *Tilmas* can be made from various materials, but even today peasants weave them of grasses and cactus fibers, which can be chewed or beaten to make them supple. Juan Diego's *tilma* was made of cactus fibers which yield a rough burlap-like material and dependably turn to dust after about twenty years.

He collected as many flowers as the *tilma* would hold and, probably shivering, hurried back down the hill to the Lady. The Lady spent some time arranging the flowers in the *tilma* in what she said was a special way. Then she bundled the *tilma* into a package, urging Juan not to disturb the arrangement and not to open the package to any other than the bishop himself.

While he was again kept waiting at the palace, some of the servants tried to snatch flowers, but as they did so the flowers seemed to meld into the sides of the *tilma* as if they were embroidered there.

Someone rushed to the bishop in amazed alarm to report that Juan should be admitted with haste. Zumárraga was consulting with a number of important people, possibly including Don Sebastián Ramírez y Fuenleal, the new governor of Mexico.

Juan Diego was quickly admitted. He may have told his story but most likely simply gave the packaged *tilma* into the suspicious hands of the bishop or allowed the *tilma* to unpackage itself. The wonderful flowers cascaded to the floor in a profusion of brilliant colors and perfumes.

Such off-season flowers in Mexico of that time could not have blossomed by any natural means at that high elevation and in that cold atmosphere. This has been investigated time and again, and where Juan Diego could have gotten the flowers by any other means has remained unknown.

Among the flowers were Castilian roses, which shocked the gathered Spanish personages, especially Bishop Zumárraga, since this variety had not yet been imported into Mexico.

Yet another electrifying shock was in store. For on the inside of the *tilma* an image now appeared — and it seems that everyone watched it appearing. Juan did not see this image at first, and when he did, he probably shouted, as the "myth" held, that the image was an exact replica of the Lady who had been appearing to him on the Tepeyac hill.

Even before the gathered personages recovered from their shock, the word of the miracle was being communicated throughout the bishop's premises and into the streets. Zumárraga, weeping, now arose and gathered Juan Diego into his arms and apparently began apologizing profusely for his former "disbelief" — insisting that Juan remain overnight as an honored guest.

Zumárraga took tender and reverent possession of the *tilma,* displaying it in his private chapel prior to transferring it to the first small chapel to be built on Tepeyac hill. Thousands of Aztecs immediately came to venerate the image — and the ominous crisis was over.

The exact reasons for the conversions, however, are not so straightforward. Atop the Tepeyac hill had once stood a temple of the great Aztec mother god Tonantzín. A rather fearsome statue of Tonantzín is found today in the elegant Anthropological Museum in Mexico City.

Tonantzín, the "Little Mother" of the earth and of corn, had been one of the most popular figures in the Aztec pantheon. It is quite credible, as has often been suggested, that the Aztecs simply accepted the apparition and the image as that of Tonantzín, called the Holy Mother Mary by the Christians.

It was to be over a hundred years before the Catholic priests could convince the converted Aztecs to cease leaving crude votive images of Tonantzín beneath the displayed *tilma.* Even today, corn, the most important staple of Mexico, is still left as a votive offering to the Virgin.

Another compelling reason for the massive conversions might be due to an apparent mix-up regarding what the Lady said she wished to be called. Zumárraga sent Juan to his home village accompanied by a retinue to guard and provide for him. There Juan Diego found his uncle, Juan Bernardino, cured and resting in the sunshine, proclaiming that the Lady had also appeared to him and told him of all that was happening. The uncle said that the Lady had told him the title by which she wished to be known in the future.

There now occurred something of a linguistic snarl, for the Lady and the two Juans spoke Nahuatl, the Aztec language, in which the letters *G* and *D* do not exist. When the Spanish interpreter listened to Juan Bernardino, he thought the man was saying, "The Ever Virgin, Holy Mary of Guadalupe." This made sense to the interpreter, because in Spain near the Guadalupe River there was a famous old Marian shrine dedicated to an early apparition of the Lady.

However, modern scholars agree that what Juan Bernardino was trying to convey was only phonetically similar to "Guadalupe." The best linguistic guesses are that Juan Bernardino was saying *tecoatlaxopeuh* — which is pronounced similarly to "Guadalupe." In any event, the Aztecs couldn't pronounce "Guadalupe" since they had no *D* or *G* sounds, and when they tried they probably said *tecoatlaxopeuh*.

In this sense, then, and as appropriately translated, the Lady wished to be called the "Entirely Perfect Virgin, Holy Mary, who will crush, stamp out, abolish, and eradicate the stone serpent." The "stone serpent" refers to the dreaded feathered serpent deity Quetzalcoatl, the most monstrous of all the Aztec gods, to whom twenty thousand human sacrifices were offered annually.

The Aztecs seemed to have taken this as a direct command from the invisible realms, and human sacrifice came to an abrupt end. By 1539, upward of eight million Aztecs had embraced the Catholic faith as a direct result of the sacred image on the *tilma*. Had the apparition not occurred both the secular and religious histories of Mexico would have been quite different.

Although the lack of early documentation regarding the apparition is a serious problem in establishing its authenticity, the *tilma* and the life-size image have been on continuous public display from December 1531 until today. It is one of the most poignant and magnetic images in the Christian world. It is unambiguously this image which has held the Mexican apparition in firm place for over 450 years. It has vigorously withstood all attempts to debunk it, and no photographs convey its astounding qualities.

It has repeatedly been scientifically determined that the *tilma* — exactly identified as ayate maguey cactus cloth, which should have decomposed 445 years ago — is still supple and vital and shows no sign of other deterioration.

It has been confirmed, though, that the image was added to at some later dates. These additions include the sunburst rays, the tassels, the cherub, the horns of the moon, the stars on the mantle, the gold edging, and the outline of the entire figure in black. These additions are composed of identifiable paint substances, and all of them show cracking and deterioration typical of age.

The robe, mantle, face, and hands, however, are composed of substances which are perfectly intact and show no signs of aging, stain, dirt, or grime — even though thousands of candles burned just beneath the image for many years until it was put behind protective glass. Infrared spectroscopy and other advanced techniques reveal no alterations of them — and reveal also that whatever the original colors are composed of it defies identification by chemical analysis.

The original substances refract light in various ways no known substance can, which serves to give the remarkable luminosity people see when looking at the image from near or far or from different angles.

Most astonishingly, close-up examination of the eyes of the image reveal reflections in their pupils which are entirely in keeping with those formed on the corneas of living human eyes. Photographs of these reflections have been computer enhanced to reveal quite recognizable faces and heads. There is no known explanation for this phenomenon, and accomplished artists, scientists, and ophthalmologists have no idea of how these eye images were achieved.

It is as if when the Aztec *tilma* was first unrolled the reflections of those present in Zumárraga's room were permanently frozen in time in the eyes of the image. Many believe one of the eye images to be that of the new Spanish governor, Ramírez y Fuenleal.

Many miraculous cures are attributed to the Virgin of Guadalupe. About twenty million people a year visit the basilica of Guadalupe to gaze in transfixed awe at the wonderful and inexplicable life-size image on Juan Diego's burlap-like *tilma*.

2

Paris, France

(1830)

Before the great 1531 appearance in Mexico there had been many reports of apparitions of the Holy Mother, some from as early as the second century. After the great apparition at Paris in 1830 there have also been many. But during the long 299-year interval between 1531 and 1830 there is hardly a trace of any apparition of the Holy Mother.

This hiatus is sometimes referred to by Marian researchers as the "dry period." No one really knows how to explain it, but two momentous factors might apply.

First, the dry period began more or less with the Protestant Reformation, which broke out in Europe in 1517 just when Hernán Cortés was preparing to conquer Mexico. The Catholic Church lost an estimated ten million adherents during the first twenty years of the Reformation. But by 1539 those losses were replaced by the conversion to the faith of more than nine million Aztecs as a direct result of the apparition in Mexico.

Second, the dry period ran concurrently with the Spanish Inquisition and the Holy Roman Inquisition. The Spanish Inquisition was established in about 1480 by the Spanish King Ferdinand and Queen Isabella — who also approved and subsidized the Columbus expedition to the New World in 1492. The Spanish Inquisition functioned as a method of secular control-by-terror in Spain, mostly to protect the monarchy and its powers and territories. It operated by secret informants and utilized anonymous reports to ruthlessly stamp out any suspected heresy or anti-monarch sentiments.

The Holy Roman Inquisition was instituted in 1549 at Rome, principally to combat the continuing effects of the Protestant Reformation and to stamp out heresy.

Since apparitions of the Holy Mother always take place outside of official religious auspices, during the Inquisitions they would have been deemed heresy or of diabolical origin. During the dry period of the apparitions, the number of those put to death in Europe by the two Inquisitions is estimated at over nine million, three-fourths of whom were women. Such terror clearly would have been a deterrent to admitting to having seen an apparition, holy or otherwise.

The Spanish Inquisition was not abolished until 1820, while the powers of the Roman Inquisition ceased only in 1829. The epoch of the great modern apparitions commenced in 1830.

The relationship in France between secular and religious authority had always been considerably different from that in Spain and the countries later comprising Italy. France was largely a Catholic nation to be sure, but one which suffered greatly because of tremendous abuses not only by the aristocracy, but by the clergy.

These matters came to a head in the violence of the French Revolution, which began in 1789. The aristocracy and church were pulled down. Thousands were murdered, and the Bourbon King Louis XVI and Queen Marie Antoinette were beheaded. Churches were defiled and burned; religious icons and statues were destroyed. Even the holy altar in Notre Dame cathedral in Paris was defecated on — and then weeks later cleaned up and converted into a temple to Venus.

Full social order was restored only by the ascension to a new throne by Napoleon Bonaparte, whose swift and fantastic military successes soon included most of Europe. Napoleon declared himself emperor in 1804. Bonaparte's empire was the most splendid since that of Charlemagne. But it crumbled to defeat by the English in 1815, and the Bourbon family was restored to the throne. The new king was the first brother of the beheaded Louis XVI, who styled himself as Louis XVIII; he was followed in 1824 by the second brother, who called himself Charles X.

The French, however, were seriously divided, and the people insisted on having some say in their government. The whole situation was quite unmanageable, and a series of political experiments and dramatic stupidities were set in motion.

A law indemnifying the nobles for lands confiscated during the great French Revolution caused a clamor of national disapproval. Enormous favors were once more conceded to the church, and popular hatred toward it arose once more. Clerics, convents, and churches were again attacked and placed in great jeopardy. Liberal journalists aided in stirring up emotions and sentiments in opposition to Charles X.

By 1830, violence and insurrections were visible everywhere. Charles X attempted to remedy this by dissolving the liberal chamber in March. In the early days of July, he and his administrators made the grave mistake of establishing new ordinances which suspended the freedom of the press.

Unprecedented social fury now arose, culminating barely two weeks after the ordinances were issued in the July Revolution of 1830. This Revolution unseated Charles X, who fled to England with his family. The throne now passed to Louis Philippe of the Bourbon secondary line, who styled himself the "Citizen King." Hatred, dissention, and discontent were everywhere, as were radical lines of thought, including budding Marxism.

One of the last things expected, though, was the sudden and strange upswing toward a return to the faith and the church. This return is mentioned in most history books, but the reasons for it are avoided by conventional historians.

During the final months of 1830, a limited edition of a new religious medal was put on sale. Its origins were cloaked in secrecy for quite some time. But miraculous cures of body, mind, and soul were quickly attributed to it, which enhanced the sales.

It was soon heard that this medal had been ordered struck during an important apparition of the Holy Mother, the first one in three hundred years. Religious officials would neither confirm nor deny this, but the hearsay brought about even larger sales of the medal.

The medal was shortly and inexplicably to become one of the all-time best-sellers of religious medals, not only in France but throughout Europe. It became a mark of renewed unity among those possessing and wearing it. In an important historical sense it served to reunite the divisive conscience of the French and helped sponsor the huge return to the faith.

The events of this holy apparition were not fully recognized by religious officials until sometime after the seer's death in 1876 — forty-six years after the apparition had occurred. This lapse of detailed information has some importance for the apparitions of 1846 and 1858 because many skeptics held that the young seers of those two apparitions were merely trying to imitate the one in 1830. But this cannot have been the case, for the apparition of 1830 was largely "secret" until after 1876. Even if anything had come into print about the apparition of 1830 before that, none of the seers at the isolated sites of the later two apparitions could read or write.

Even though the details were missing for some time, there was gossip that an apparition had occurred to a nun within the seminary of the Sisters of Charity at 140 rue du Bac in Paris. Pilgrims began arriving.

The apparition occurred to a postulant nun named Catherine Labouré. Just two years after Napoleon had made himself emperor of the French, Catherine was born on May 2, 1806, in the tiny village of Fain-les-Moutiers not far from Dijon. Although her father, who had been educated to be a priest, and her mother, a former schoolmistress, were above the educational average, Catherine seems to have had little interest in study or world affairs.

Her father had ultimately elected to be a farmer rather than a priest, because he detested religious institutions and popery. Portraits of Pierre and Madeleine Labouré show them as cultured. They had fifteen or seventeen children (depending on the sources), of whom ten lived beyond infancy; of the ten, Catherine was the ninth.

Catherine's mind was not average. Some sources indicate that she remained "strangely uneducated." Other sources, more directly to the point, indicate that her learning aptitudes were "truly abysmal" and that her "stupidity" was the butt of cruel ridicule by her schoolmates.

On the other hand, if Catherine did not learn or interact with her peers in average ways, she took over the running of the entire Labouré household when she was nine. Whether this was before or after her mother's death is not clear. Why the ninth of ten living children should take over the household is not clear either.

Sometime after her mother's death, it seems that at least part of the large family was broken up. Catherine then seems to have been passed around to relatives.

At an early age she had asked her father for permission to become a nun, but she was sternly refused because of his anti-clerical sentiments. Some sources indicate that Catherine eventually turned down three marriage proposals, but others omit reference to these altogether. She undertook to follow her religious calling despite her father's objections.

While laboring in a restaurant she applied to enter the Sisters of Charity at Chantillon. But the sister superior was "most reluctant" to admit one so "poorly educated" or "stupid" and probably even more reluctant because her obstinate and anti-clerical father refused to extend the dower customarily expected of those entering the sisterhood. Somehow these difficulties were overcome, and on April 21, 1830, Catherine, now twenty-four, was received as a postulant and directed to the seminary at the rue du Bac in Paris.

Catherine was barely established in her postulant's duties of scrubbing floors and dealing with slops when she was required to be present in the procession to move the bodily remains of St. Vincent de Paul, the community's founder, from the Cathedral of Notre Dame to the motherhouse of the Lazarites, founded by the saint.

She promptly claimed to a number of other sisters to have seen the "heart" of St. Vincent de Paul glowing above a display case in the seminary containing some of his relics.

For this claim she apparently received what today we would call "counseling" from her superiors at the seminary. One Father Aladel, either her "advisor" or "confessor" (both terms are used in the records), indicated that she was at the seminary to learn how "to serve the poor, not to dream."

Whether Father Aladel was her confessor or advisor is of some factual interest regarding the attempts at secrecy that eventually came to surround the apparition. If confessor, he would be forbidden to reveal her confession to anyone. If advisor at the seminary, he would have been obliged to inform the director superior.

In any event, and in spite of Father Aladel's warnings, it seems Catherine made no secret of the fact that she fervently wished to see the Virgin Mary, and she prayed openly for this grace. All this is unusual behavior for a postulant newly entering the Sisters of Charity. Obedience, submissive behavior, and self-imposed humility would have been more the case and, in fact, even insisted upon.

Just three months after she had entered the seminary as a postulant, she went to bed on the night of July 18, 1830, the eve of the feast of St. Vincent de Paul—convinced, as she seems to have told everyone who would listen, that this holy patron would help her obtain this high wish. July 18 was just nine days before the July Revolution of 1830 and just after the July ordinances which silenced the press.

At about 11:30 p.m., Catherine was awakened, having heard her name called three times. In her room, she saw a "child of four or five years, with shimmering golden hair, enveloped in a golden light, and dressed all in white." Various accounts exist as to what happened next; from them I've reconstructed the following. "Get up," said the child. "My Sister! My Sister! Come quickly to the chapel. The Blessed Virgin awaits you there [La Sainte Vierge vous attend!]."

Catherine later stated to Father Aladel that she was confused and troubled, and asked the child how she could get through the seminary's dark hallways to the chapel without waking the other sisters. "Don't be afraid," replied the child, "everyone is asleep. I'll go with you."

Catherine followed him through the corridors. Along the way "the lights" (assuredly candles) lit up, which astonished her. All of the accounts agree that the child kept to her left just ahead, and he himself was surrounded with rays of light.

The chapel door opened by itself, and the interior was lit up everywhere "as if for midnight Mass."

Catherine did not see the Blessed Virgin anywhere in the chapel, but the child led her to the sanctuary, to the side of the director's chair, where they waited. (The chair is preserved at the seminary.) Catherine was nervous and apprehensive that the night warders would discover and punish her.

At midnight Catherine recounted that she "heard a noise like the rustling of a silk dress or layers of billowing silk skirts. I saw a lady," she said, "who was seating herself in the [director's] chair on the altar steps" who looked more like a "fine lady than a saint."

"Here," said the child, "is the Blessed Virgin; here she is!" Catherine stated that she did not recognize this lady as the Blessed Virgin. But the child seemed "to have read her thoughts" and, "his voice changing into that of a grown man," reaffirmed that the lady was indeed the Blessed Virgin.

While Catherine was still perplexed, the Lady began speaking. Most of the records are consistent concerning what the Lady said, largely because Catherine's principal historian, Jules Chevalier, later provided the officially accepted version. The Lady began:

My child, the good God wishes to charge you with a mission. You will have much to suffer, but you will rise above these sufferings by reflecting that what you do is for the glory of God. You will be tormented until you have told him who is charged with directing you [either Father Aladel or the superior director or both]. You will be contradicted; but do not fear, you will have grace. Tell with confidence all that passes here and within you. Tell it simply. Do not be afraid.

"The times are very evil," the Lady now went on. "Sorrows will befall France, the throne will [again] be overturned, the whole world will soon be plunged into every kind of misery." At this point, the Lady became very distressed, but she continued:

'But come now to the foot of the altar. There graces will be shed on all, great or small, who fervently ask for them. Grave troubles are coming. There will be great danger, for this [the seminary] and other [religious] communities. At one moment when the danger is acute, everyone will believe all to be lost; you will recall my visit and [this seminary] will have the protection of God. But it will not be the same for other communities.

Tears then appeared in the Lady's eyes.

Among the clergy of Paris there will be victims — Monseigneur the Archbishop [tears come afresh], my child, the cross will be treated with contempt, they will hurl it to the ground and trample it. Blood will flow. The streets will run with blood. Monseigneur the Archbishop will be stripped of his garments [here the Lady is in anguish and cannot speak for a time].

During this interlude Catherine "wondered when all this would take place." She found she "knew." Some of the events would take place soon, others "in about forty years [1870]."

The Lady now continued: "My eyes will be ever upon you. I shall grant you graces. Special graces will be given to all who ask them, but people must pray."

At this point the apparition disappeared "like a cloud that had evaporated." The child led her back to her bed. The clock struck 2:00 a.m.

The next morning (July 19) Catherine said that she had seen the Blessed Virgin, although whom she told is not clear from the sources. A discrepancy is apparent in that some of the sources say she told Father Aladel, identified as her confessor; but if so, then as her confessor he was bound never to tell anyone else — which apparently he quickly did. It's quite likely, though, that she (or Father Aladel) would have told the superior director of the seminary, as directed by the Lady, but the sources here are inconsistent.

It is certain that she told someone, and that "someone" forbid her to tell anyone else. This prohibition seems not to have done much good, for a number of people at the seminary told others that the Virgin had appeared to someone in the seminary, a secret no one was supposed to know about, but about which everyone soon did.

On the other hand, it would also be logical that the inhabitants of the seminary at first concluded that they had a mentally deranged postulant on their hands.

In any event, the records (at least those later officially endorsed) indicate that this event was kept "secret" and that the seer was kept "anonymous." Some sources say that Father Aladel again condemned her "illusions" and said, "If you want to honor Our Lady, imitate her virtues and guard yourself against imagination."

But if disbelief, secrecy, and anonymity at first prevailed, they soon began to unravel. Predictions that are fulfilled are certain to help validate an apparition's authenticity. The Lady had predicted on the night of July 18–19 that "the throne will again be overturned." King Charles X was dethroned eight days later on July 26–28 during the "Glorious Three Days" which became known as the July Revolution of 1830.

The predicted "grave troubles" surfaced in the form of barricades thrown up on the streets of Paris, riots broke out in Paris and elsewhere, and many were slaughtered. Marauders broke into churches, crucifixes were hauled out, broken, and defecated and urinated upon. As the Lady had predicted, "Monseigneur the Archbishop [Archbishop de Quelen]" was beaten, forcibly stripped nearly naked of his garments, and twice had to flee for his life.

Additionally, and again as predicted, the seminary of the Sisters of Charity on the rue du Bac was surrounded by angry mobs and fired upon, while other religious buildings were burned or destroyed. But, as promised by the Lady, the terrified inhabitants at the rue du Bac seminary remained otherwise unharmed.

Some later critics held that these predictions were conveniently made in retrospect. But something at this point has to account for why Catherine was not just shipped off to a place where the church placed mentally disturbed postulants — and account, as well, for almost immediate shifts in attitudes toward her.

If the predictions truly had been made just days before their fulfillment, then they would have made a great impression on the seminary officials, who doubtlessly would have reported them to the archbishop. The predictions were certainly in hand as of 1831, and by 1870 all of the predictions given during the first apparition in 1830 had come true.

Catherine "knew" that some of the "grave troubles" referring to "Monseigneur the Archbishop" would take place soon, but other of the predictions in "about forty years." During the "grave troubles" of yet another revolution of 1848, another archbishop, Monseigneur Affre, was shot to death at the barricades.

In 1870, forty years later, the cross was again "trampled on," and Monseigneur Darboy, then archbishop of Paris, was murdered at the onset of the Franco-Prussian War. These events fulfilled the predictions Catherine had said the Lady had given her — except for those pertaining to the "whole world."

In any event, Catherine was not shipped off in 1830. Rather, she was sworn to secrecy, to which she apparently agreed. This procedure was not unusual in convents and monasteries when unusual phenomena took place. However, the procedure was designed not to indicate the authenticity of an apparition, but to reinforce humility, eradicate pride, and prevent veneration of unusual phenomena that some might interpret as being holy.

But secrecy, rather than punishment or hospitalization, is a clear indication that the holy event had been accepted as such by Catherine's superiors as of August 1830.

During the course of the first apparition, Catherine had been told that she was to have a mission. But it was not until four months later when the Lady returned that she found out what it was to be.

During this second apparition, the Lady appeared in a guise and dress quite different from the first. In Catherine's own words, or words attributed to her:

On November 27, 1830, which fell on the Saturday before the first Sunday of Advent, at five-thirty in the evening...I heard a sound like the rustling of a silk dress, from the tribune near the picture of St. Joseph.

Turning in that direction, I saw the Blessed Virgin [floating] at the level of the picture. The Virgin was standing. She was of medium height, and clothed all in white.

Her dress was of the whiteness of the dawn, made in the style called "a la Vierge" — that is, high neck and plain sleeves. A white veil covered her head and fell [down to] either side of her feet. Under the veil her hair, in coils, was bound with a fillet ornamented with lace.... Her face was sufficiently exposed, indeed exposed very well, and so beautiful that it seemed to me impossible to express her ravishing beauty.

Her feet rested on a white globe, that is to say, half globe, or at least I saw only half. There was also a serpent, green in color with yellow spots.

A frame, slightly oval in shape, formed around the Blessed Virgin. Within it was written in letters of gold: "O Mary, conceived without sin, pray for us who have recourse to thee."

The inscription, in a semi-circle, began at the height of the right hand, passed over the head, and finished at the height of the left hand. The hands [now] were raised to the height of the stomach and held, in a very relaxed manner as if offering it to God, a golden ball surmounted with a little golden cross, which represented the world. Her eyes were not raised to heaven, now lowered. Her face was of such beauty that I could not describe it.

All at once I saw rings on her fingers, three rings to each finger, the largest one near the base of the finger, one of medium size in the middle, the smallest one at the tip. Each ring was set with gems, some more beautiful than others; the larger gems emitted greater rays and the smaller gems, smaller rays; the rays bursting from all sides flooded the base, so that I could no longer see the feet of the Blessed Virgin.

At this moment, while I was contemplating her, the Blessed Virgin lowered her eyes and looked at me. I heard a voice speaking these words: "This ball that you see represents the whole world, especially France, and each person in particular." I could not express what I felt at this, what I saw, the beauty and the brilliance of the dazzling rays. "They [the rays] are the symbols of the graces I shed upon those who ask for them. The gems from which rays do not fall are the graces which souls forget to ask."

The golden ball disappeared in the brilliance of the sheaves of light bursting from all sides; the hands turned out and the arms were bent down under the weight of the treasures of grace obtained.

Then the voice said: "Have a medal struck after this model. All who wear it will receive great graces; they should wear it around the neck. Graces will abound for those who wear it with confidence."

At this instant the tableau seemed to me to turn, and I beheld the reverse of the medal: a large M surmounted by a bar and a cross; beneath the M were the Hearts of Jesus and Mary, the one crowned with thorns, the other pierced with a sword.

At this point, the apparition disappeared "like a candle blown out." Many later artistic renderings of this apparition do not include the white veil, but do include a blue garment around the shoulders and arms not mentioned in Catherine's description.

This form of the apparition of the Holy Mother to Catherine was repeated exactly either four or five times. The last was in January 1831, during which the Lady indicated that Catherine would see her no more but would often hear "my voice in your prayers."

The official records state that Father Aladel was not told of the second and subsequent apparitions because he wasn't interested — which leads to the question of who was told, which is nowhere mentioned in my sources.

But somewhere between the second apparition and February 1832 Father Aladel became involved again. And in May he permitted one Monsieur Vachette to strike the first of the medals in the number of two thousand.

This act on Father Aladel's part relates to the number of people who knew the details of this "secret" apparition. It is completely understandable that Father Aladel would not take upon himself the responsibility of creating a *religious artifact* before he explained why to his superiors. The production of the medal must have required the agreement of the director general of the Sisters of Charity and at least the tacit approval of Archbishop de Quelen. But this would mean that the "secrecy" of the apparitional events and the identity of Catherine as the seer were not kept as an in-house seminary secret. Moreover, the medal was struck *before* later official inquiries were convened to establish the circumstances of its origin, and again these inquiries would have involved the staff of the archbishopric.

The Sisters of Charity soon began giving the medal to the sick and poor who were being cared for by them. It clearly was understood that the medal was from a holy source. Conversions and miracle cures were soon reported by some of these patients, and the medal was thereafter known as the Miraculous Medal. Similar healings and conversions have occurred ever since.

Some accounts hold that the medal was not again reproduced until several years after the apparitions. But other documents accepted as official indicate that within the next two years (1832–33), fifty thousand were struck and given away or sold. In France five hundred thousand more had been sold by the autumn of 1834, two million by 1836, a million a year thereafter, and more than a *billion* had been sold worldwide by the time of Catherine's death in December 1876.

Officially accepted records indicate that the first inquiries regarding the apparition's authenticity were not undertaken until 1836, but the medal had been approved for circulation in 1832, and by 1836 about two million had been sold.

Thus, in spite of the plans for secrecy surrounding the apparition and its seer, the story simply had to be told with each of the Miraculous Medals. During the next few years, the only remaining "secret" aspect of the apparition seems to have been the name of the seer.

Postulant Catherine Labouré, who openly had wished to see the Holy Virgin, became Sister Catherine on January 30, 1831, shortly after the last appearance of the Holy Mother. She was immediately assigned to work as a cook in the sisterhood's hospice of Enghien in the city of Reuilly.

The Holy Mother's vehicle lived at that hospice in that occupation for the next forty-six years. Her circumstances were humble, but she apparently made no effort to better them. She maintained a self-imposed silence about the apparition.

This silence was so strict that when in 1836 the archbishop of Paris urged her to come to Paris and testify in person at the first official inquiry, she repeatedly asked to be excused on the astonishing grounds that she could not remember the details of the apparition. She never testified.

This is almost certain proof positive that before 1836, Catherine had already been officially accepted as a vehicle of the Holy Mother, since the archbishop could easily have demanded her presence under pain of punishment, even of excommunication. He did not, nor did anyone else pressure her.

Just before her peaceful death on December 31, 1876, Catherine was asked to confirm that it had indeed been she who had seen "la Sainte Vierge." And she did.

In 1895, the Miraculous Medal was accorded a Mass and office of its own within the Roman Catholic liturgy. Catherine's childhood home was preserved as a museum.

In 1933, the process of exhumation was performed on Catherine's long-buried body, which was "found incorrupt by medical examination with the eyes still blue" (upon death the eyes always quickly turn dark and decompose). The incorruption of a seer's body long after death is automatically accepted as testament that the seer was especially chosen by divine will.

Catherine's body was moved to the chapel of the seminary on the rue de Bac, where for a while it could be viewed behind glass. Today the body is enclosed just beneath the altar built upon the spot where the Holy Mother first appeared in the seminary chapel. An average of more than a thousand visitors a day come there in wonderment and veneration.

In 1947, Catherine Labouré was proclaimed St. Catherine Labouré by Pope Pius XII. One of the chief forms of veneration of this saint is the Perpetual Novena (conducted weekly) in honor of Our Lady of the Miraculous Medal. Established in 1930 in Philadelphia, it has since then been observed in more than five thousand churches and chapels throughout the world.

The great apparition of 1531 in Mexico produced her own artifact, a life-size image of herself. The great apparition of 1830 *designed* an artifact and asked human beings to produce it. Both artifacts were tremendously influential.

3

La Salette, France
(1846)

As we have seen, the July Revolution of 1830 took place just days after the Holy Mother's first appearance to Catherine Labouré. That revolution placed Louis Philippe on the throne of France. And as the Lady had predicted, the "sorrows [which] will befall France" began with renewed vigor.

Even though Louis Philippe styled himself the "Citizen King" of the First Republic, his regime soon turned out to be a frank plutocracy, a government run by the wealthy bourgeoisie. The French conquered Algeria by 1838, signaling a return of French "glory." This was Louis Philippe's single high point — in the eyes of the French anyway, but not so much of the Algerians.

After 1838, the regime became increasingly autocratic and money-grabbing, disregarding the plights of the new urban proletariat and the nation's farmers. And so the citizens of the "Citizen King" began suffering.

As the year 1846 dawned, however, few suspected that a great economic depression would come down on the French, for most felt France to be vital in spite of its political difficulties. Least of all, none even dreamed that another Napoleon could come into power in France. Yet, by the end of the year France was electrified by the news that an apparition of the Holy Mother had occurred — during which the Lady had predicted as much through the mouths of two illiterate children.

The isolated hamlet of La Salette is found far to the southeast of Paris high in the French Alps. Life there was hard and poor and frugal, and had been so for centuries. So the increasing turmoil elsewhere in France probably had little meaning for the inhabitants.

It is doubtful that the 1830 apparition in Paris was known about in La Salette, since the details of that apparition were still a closely guarded secret. And there is very little reason to think that the inhabitants of the La Salette area were politically up to date or even cared very much about the shifts in French history, which occurred very quickly. Nor is there any reason to think that any of the young, illiterate children in La Salette would have been very much aware of anything outside their daily routines.

Late in the afternoon of Saturday, September 19, 1846, two excited children, who had been hired to guard cows grazing on the mountain slopes, returned with the cows to the hamlet of Ablandins not far from La Salette. They said that a "beautiful Lady" had appeared to them in a circle of light more brilliant than the sun.

With this sighting began one of the larger tumults in apparitional history. The two young seers of the apparition were a fourteen-year-old girl named Melanie Mathieu (according to some sources) or fifteen-year-old Melanie Calvat (according to others); and Maximin Giraud, whom all sources agree was eleven. All sources also agree that both came from poor families, that they were illiterate, and that they spoke only the local dialect of their region of France.

Melanie is said to have been one of eight children and had been sent out to beg while still a small child. Maximin is described as a "troubled boy" who spent much time knocking about in the streets, where he too begged or connived or stole something to eat.

Both were natives of Corps, a small town about three miles

down the mountain slopes from La Salette. But they had not met until Friday, September 18, 1846, when they were jointly hired to guard cattle on the mountain slopes, having obtained this minuscule employment from two local farmers of Ablandins, another nearby hamlet.

It would appear, then, that Melanie and Maximin had known each other for less than twenty-four hours when on Saturday, September 19, 1846, the apparition occurred. This remarkable appearance was to come under vehement attack by skeptics who said that the children invented their story. Other critics held, and some continue to do so today, that what the children actually saw was a deranged old woman who liked to dress up as the Blessed Virgin and parade herself along the mountain slopes.

It seems that this mad woman did exist. But still, neither she nor the twenty-four hours are sufficient to explain how the astonishing intricacies of the apparition could be constructed. For example, even if by some slim chance all three had heard something of the political events in France, it was completely impossible for them to have invented the Lady's warnings of future environmental hazards to our planet which were described in detail by the Lady and are completely recognizable *today.*

In any event, during the latter part of that Saturday afternoon, when it was time to return with the cows to Ablandins, in a ravine where they had earlier rested to eat their packed-along lunch, the two seers had come upon a large circle of brilliant light "outshining the sun." As they watched "fear-stricken," the light intensified and expanded. As they were about to flee, the brilliant circle "opened," and gradually both of the seers could make out "the figure of a woman." She was seated, her face in her hands, and was weeping.

There is some difficulty in establishing what the two seers saw next, because no one seems to have recorded their statements until some time after the event. It was Melanie's version which was recorded for posterity, with Maximin confirming it.

Almost without doubt, Melanie's description of the apparition underwent several successive elaborations as she grew older and was perhaps helped in constructing them. In these we find "the woman" already referred to at the beginning of her recorded text as the "Most Holy Virgin."

But in that text, "the woman" is described as wearing a "yellow pinafore," which was and still is totally uncharacteristic of the traditional image of the Virgin Mary. So immediate recognition by the seers of the apparition seems unlikely.

Most of the earlier sources agree that at first the Lady was not recognized as the Holy Mother. Indeed, the next day the two seers were twice taken to the spot of the apparition by groups interrogating them. One of those interrogators was Mayor Peytard of Ablandins, who was cross-questioning the two seers and threatening them with jail if they didn't cooperate. During those interrogations, the two seers did not identify the Lady as the Blessed Virgin. Melanie is quoted as saying: "Perhaps she was a great saint" and, even later, "If we had known it was a great saint, we would have asked her to take us with her."

Melanie's description appears later to have been widely accepted and utilized, although there are other sources differing in arrangement and details. The source I depend on was first published in English in 1854 by the Most Reverend William Ullathorne, archbishop of Birmingham, England, who went to La Salette in 1853–54 especially to investigate the events there. In 1853, the archbishop found that the apparition by then had been accepted as one of the Blessed Virgin for some time. According to Melanie, confirmed by Maximin:

> *The clothing of the Most Holy Virgin was silver white and quite brilliant. It was quite intangible. It was made up of light and glory, sparkling and dazzling. There is no expression nor comparison to be found on earth. The Most Holy Virgin had a yellow pinafore.*
>
> *What am I saying, yellow? She had a pinafore more brilliant than several suns put together. It was not of tangible material; it was composed of glory, and this glory was scintillating, and ravishingly beautiful.*

The Most Holy Virgin had two chains, one a little wider than the other. From the narrower hung the cross. These chains — since they must be given the name of chains — were like rays of brightly shining glory, sparkling and dazzling.

Her shoes — since they must be called shoes — were white, but a silvery brilliant white. There were roses around them. These roses were dazzlingly beautiful, and from the heart of each rose there shone forth a flame of very beautiful and pleasing light. On her shoes there was a buckle of gold, not the gold of this earth, but rather the gold of paradise.

The crown of roses which she had placed on her head was so beautiful, so brilliant, that it defies imagination. The different colored roses were not of this earth; it was a joining together of flowers which crowned the head of the Most Holy Virgin.

But the roses kept changing and replacing each other, and then, from the heart of each rose there shone a beautiful entrancing light, which gave the roses a shimmering beauty. From the crown of roses there seemed to arise golden branches with a number of other little flowers mingled with the shining ones. The whole thing formed a most beautiful diadem.

The Most Holy Virgin was tall and well proportioned. She seemed so light that a mere breath could have stirred her, yet she was motionless and perfectly balanced. Her face was majestic, imposing. The voice of the Beautiful Lady was soft. It was enchanting, ravishing, warming to the ears.

The eyes of the majestic Mary appeared thousands of times more beautiful than the rarest brilliants, diamonds, and precious stones. They shone like two suns; [but] they were soft, softness itself, as clear as a mirror.

In her eyes, you could see paradise. They drew you to her; she seemed to want to draw and give herself.

The Holy Virgin was surrounded by two lights [auras]. The first light, the nearer to the Most Holy Virgin, reached as far as us [Melanie and Maximin]. It shone most beautifully and scintillatingly. The second light shone out a little around

*the Beautiful Lady and we found ourselves bathed [included]
in it. It was motionless, that is to say, that it wasn't scintillating, but much more brilliant than our poor sun on earth.
All this light did not harm nor tire the eyes in any way.*

*In addition to all these lights, all this splendor, there shone
forth concentrations or beams of light and single rays of light
from the body of the Holy Virgin, from her clothes and from
all over her.*

*The Holy Virgin had a most pretty cross hanging around
her neck. This cross seemed golden — I say golden rather
than gold plated, for I have sometimes seen objects which
were golden with varying shades of gold — which had a
much more beautiful effect on my eyes than simple gold
plate.*

*On this shining, beautiful cross, there was a Christ; it
was Our Lord on the Cross. Near both ends of the cross
there was a hammer, and at the other end, a pair of tongs.
The Christ was skin-colored, but He shone dazzlingly; and
the light that shone forth from His whole body seemed like
brightly shining darts which pierced my heart with the desire
to melt inside Him.*

*At times, the Christ appeared to be dead. His head was
bent forward and His body seemed to give way, as if about
to fall, had He not been held back by the nails which held
Him to the Cross.*

*At other times, the Christ appeared to be alive. His head
was erect, His eyes open, and He seemed to be on the cross
of His own accord.*

*The Holy Virgin was crying nearly the whole time she was
speaking to us. Her tears flowed gently, one by one, down
to her knees, then, like sparks of light, they disappeared.
They were glittering and full of love. I would have liked to
comfort her and stop her tears.*

✴

The apparition at La Salette occurred only once, during the afternoon of September 16, 1846. The seers insisted that the Lady first spoke French to them. They spoke only the patois of the region in which they lived. When the weeping Lady realized the two children were not understanding French, she thereafter spoke in the patois.

Even then the seers said that they had trouble both understanding and keeping up with what she was saying, but that "pictures" arose in their minds. It seems that the Lady presented her messages both verbally in the patois and made the seers see appropriate images in some form.

The Lady enunciated a clear and concise prediction that referred to forthcoming agricultural and economic conditions. After some initial confusion, the weeping Lady finally said:

> *You do not understand, my children. I will tell it to you another way. If the harvest is spoiled, it does not [yet] seem to affect you. I made you see this last year with the potatoes. They [the potatoes] will continue to go bad and [by] Christmas [1846] there will be none left.*
>
> *If you have corn, you must not sow it. The beasts will eat all that you sow. And all that grows will fall to dust when you thresh it. A great famine will come. Before the famine comes, children under the age of seven will begin to tremble and will die in the arms of those who hold them. The others will do penance through hunger. The nuts will be bad; the grapes will become rotten.*

Having predicted this much, the Lady then launched into a long apocalyptic statement which dealt with the future. The children said they didn't understand the words very much, but that the Lady caused relevant pictures to form in their heads.

These pictures seemed to have become indelibly etched in the seers' minds, since they could independently call them up throughout their lives and describe them again and again in the same way.

The news that the Holy Mother had appeared on the barren slopes of La Salette was quickly communicated down the mountains and gradually throughout all France. Pilgrims and the curious began arriving, first in small groups, but in increasing volume barely four weeks later. Soon the hamlets of Ablandins, Corps, La Salette, and all the nearby houses and farms were overrun.

Printed sheets and pamphlets were available by the middle of October 1846 which included the first interviews of the two young seers, descriptions of the event, the predictions, and the lengthy apocalyptic statement or extracts from it.

These clearly establish that the prediction of famine was in print by October, prior to the somber events that came to fulfill it. By the end of 1846, around Christmas, all of the elements of the prediction had begun to be fulfilled. Abysmal secular economic and political situations engulfed France. The wealthy merchants began withholding produce to drive up prices, which the average citizen could not afford.

An unanticipated onset of dreadful diseases also occurred — attacking food products, animals, and humans as well. By Christmas potatoes could not be bought at all; they had rotted in the ground. Shortly thereafter corn began to rot; at first it was thought good only for animal feed — until the cattle bloated and died from eating it.

The walnut crop failed. The grape crop, of vast importance to France, was attacked by Phylloxera. In many areas intense famine ensued, from which the many poorer regions of France suffered horribly. A form of cholera struck many regions, causing a brief attack of shaking and sickness before almost certain death. Children were especially susceptible, and thousands died, in some cases entire families.

Hardly anything resembling the intensity of this misfortune had occurred before. Even the most cynical doubters of the apparition were forced (and still are) to acknowledge the astonishing accuracy of the Lady's predictions.

�֎

By January 1847, the authenticity of the apparition began to be accepted. Now began the massive and arduous treks of pilgrims into the high French Alps, and the trek into history of the apparition itself.

Some critics held that what we would today call the local "chamber of commerce" saw advantages in having a holy apparition in their area to attract pilgrims and thus bolster the local economy. That economy did pick up, of course. The critics accused the conspirators of producing the spring that appeared at the exact spot of the apparition.

But a bottle of its water was brought to a seriously ill woman who drank of it a little each day, and nine days later she quit her bed, her health perfectly restored. Increasing numbers of pilgrims soon arrived to drink the water, and possibly many in the area did also.

The apparition also called forth legions of skeptics and critics. Unlike the apparition in Paris in 1830, which was handled very discretely, the apparition at La Salette was subjected to vociferous attacks and denunciations. The two young seers were aggressively interviewed, called liars and cheats, and threatened with imprisonment and excommunication, although neither comprehended exactly what excommunication was. They were besieged by reporters who found their way up into the French Alps, while devout pilgrims begged "favors" from them. Some of the curious taunted them, and a few rocks were thrown.

Meanwhile, the environs of La Salette, Ablandins, and Corps were soon completely submerged by hundreds and then thousands of pilgrims. In short order, the resulting fracas required an investigation. To get the preliminaries under way, Bishop de Bruillard sent along one Father Chambon, superior of the Grenoble minor seminary, and three other members of its faculty. The report of this investigation was given to the bishop in November 1846.

This again establishes that within about two months of September 1846, the apparition had gained ever-widening prominence — *before* the ominous predictions started to be fulfilled in December 1846.

Because of this early report in November, Bishop de Bruillard appointed two more commissions to examine the known facts independently of each other. These two commissions, strenuously "testing" the two seers, were apparently working along when the predictions of famine and disease were fulfilled abundantly.

The awful fulfillments of the predictions together with many more pilgrims arriving in the area in the spring of 1847 led to more commissions being set up. By September 1847 thousands of pilgrims had overflowed all the accommodations in the mountain hamlets. By the eve of the first anniversary of the apparition, many hundreds of newcomers had to sleep in the open.

By this time, twenty-three cures had been claimed (with hundreds more to follow). This development required a new commission of sixteen, then twenty investigators, as well as "observation" of the two seers by the Sisters of Providence at Corps.

By the end of 1847, the apparition at La Salette was big news throughout France, and the news had also reached the College of Cardinals and Pope Pius IX at Rome. Thus it developed that the children were "pressured" to write out the secrets entrusted to them by the Blessed Virgin so that these might be transmitted to the pope. But from what can be established about the educational levels of the children, we can conclude that neither could write, certainly not in French, Italian, or Latin.

What the two seers dictated was finally delivered in sealed envelopes to the pope by a Father Rousselot and a Father Gerin in 1851. The result was the "gratifying acceptance" of the apparition by cardinals, bishops, and the pope.

The "facts" of the apparition were further examined by Cardinal Lambruschini in Rome, and in early 1852 diocesan authorities finally announced that "nothing less than an apparition of the Blessed Virgin had been seen by two herders on September 19, 1846."

In May of 1852, in the presence of more than ten thousand people, Bishop de Bruillard made the ascent of the mountain at La Salette and laid the cornerstone of a new basilica on the site of the apparition, a desolate area surrounded only by barren alpine slopes.

It must be noted that all of this constituted only unofficial approval. Veneration of Our Lady of La Salette was not officially approved until one hundred years later on September 19, 1946, the centenary of Our Lady of La Salette, sometimes also known as the Madonna of Tears.

The apocalypse of Our Lady of La Salette is very interesting. But it is also long, and so here I provide only extracts. It was, and still is, an unpopular apocalypse — for the Lady, whom we can see was unhappy, launched it with these words:

> *The priests, ministers of my Son, the priests, by their wicked lives, by their irreverence and their impiety in the celebration of the holy mysteries, by their love of money, their love of honors and pleasures, the priests have become cesspools of impurity. Yes, the priests are asking vengeance, and vengeance is hanging over their heads.*

This passage of the apocalypse has not, of course, been received very well by the "ministers of my Son," which probably explains why it is often deleted from published accounts of the apparition. In future apparitions the Lady repeated this complaint. After more along those lines, the Lady continued:

> *God will strike in an unprecedented way. Woe to the inhabitants of the earth! ... The chiefs, the leaders of the people of God have neglected prayer and penance, and the devil has dimmed their intelligence.... God will allow the old serpent to cause divisions among those who reign in every society and in every family. Physical and moral agonies will be suffered. God will abandon mankind to itself and will send punishments which will follow one after the other.... The society of men is on the eve of the most terrible scourges and of gravest events. Mankind must expect ... to drink from the chalice of the wrath of God.*

At this point most analysts mention the horrible Franco-Prussian war, World Wars I and II, and the rise of Communism — "most terrible scourges" which altogether account for the loss of upward of a billion lives.

Having thus chastised deplorable religious and secular situations, the Lady then moved on to a French political matter:

May the curate of my Son, Pope Pius IX, never leave Rome again after 1859;...I will be at his side. May he be on his guard against Napoleon: he is two-faced, and when he wishes to make himself pope as well as emperor, God will soon draw back from him.

This passage needs explaining since it contains an important prediction. Pope Pius IX had been elected early in 1846. In that year, the year of the apparition, no one could have imagined *another* Napoleon arising in France, much less another Emperor Napoleon.

Indeed, the only possible successor to the great Napoleon was his nephew, who lived in relative obscurity. Those who knew him, or could remember his existence, considered him a vain and stupid idiot, and it was completely unthinkable that he would ascend anywhere.

This passage must have been laughed at. It was therefore a shock when the vain idiot was elected president of France in December 1848 during the famine — and in November 1852 became Emperor Napoleon III with full dictatorial powers.

Regarding Pope Pius IX, in 1848, two years after his election to the papacy, political confusion and rioting drove him from Rome to Gaeta. He returned to Rome in 1850 to be supported in power only by the arms of the new Napoleon.

It was during 1851 that this pontiff received the apocalypse from La Salette. This passage must have immeasurably impressed the pontiff, and everyone else as well. Ultimately, there was also some truth regarding the matter of Napoleon III wishing to take over the papacy — in almost exactly the same way that his famous uncle, Napoleon I, had considered doing. If the Lady's predictions about famine and disease had been impressive, those about Napoleon III were breathtaking when they came to pass.

No one was any longer laughing at the La Salette apocalypse.

Although in the past other apparitions of the Virgin Mary had delivered apocalypses, all of them had been more or less lost in garbled myth or oblivion. The world, then, had not encountered a full-fledged Marian apocalypse for many hundreds of years.

As time went on, many critics said that the La Salette apocalypse became increasingly irrelevant. Toward the end of the apocalypse narrative the Lady forewarned of very ominous things to come. Those forewarnings must have been completely unintelligible at the time and for decades thereafter, which accounts for why they are often omitted in published versions. Bear in mind that the following was a part of the apocalypse in 1846. Until the late 1960s there existed no reality to which these predictions corresponded. In reading the following, think of ecology, atmospheric pollution, AIDS and Ebola, the stratospheric rise of crime, mind pollution: indeed, think of our overall situation today. In 1846, the apparition at La Salette warned about the future:

> *The earth will be struck by calamities of all kinds, in addition to plague and famine which will be widespread. There will be a series of wars until the last war....Before this comes to pass, there will he a kind of false peace in the world. People will think of nothing but amusement. The wicked will give themselves over to all kinds of sin....But blessed are the souls humbly guided by the Holy Spirit! I shall fight at their side until they reach the fullness of years.*

Here we must envision being in the pictures the Lady is causing to form in the minds of the two seers. Her words are describing what is being shown to them:

> *Nature is asking for vengeance because of man, and she trembles with dread at what must happen to the earth*

*stained with crime. Tremble, earth,...and you who pro-
claim yourselves as serving Jesus Christ and who, on the
inside, only adore yourselves, tremble....*

*The seasons will be altered. The earth will produce noth-
ing but bad fruit. The stars will lose their regular motion.
The moon will only reflect a faint reddish glow.*

*Water and fire will give the earth's glove [the atmos-
phere, our planet's magnetic field?] convulsions and terrible
earthquakes which will swallow up mountains, cities.... The
demons of the air...will perform awful wonders on earth
in the atmosphere, and men will become more and more
perverted.*

*Woe to the inhabitants of earth! There will be bloody
wars and famines, plagues and infectious diseases.... Men
will beat their heads against walls, call for their [own] death,
and death will be their torment.*

*There will be thunderstorms which will shake cities, earth-
quakes which will swallow up countries...the sun is darkening...the abyss is opening....*

*Who will be the victor if God does not shorten the length
of the test?...And then water and fire will purge the earth
and consume all the works of men's pride [after which] all
will be renewed.*

God will be served and glorified.

As for the two young seers of the Madonna of Tears, as they grew
up they poured oil into skeptical fires by not becoming humble as
is expected of chosen vehicles of the Holy Mother. Indeed, Maximin Girard became vain about his celebrity status, strutted about
importantly, and was often drunk, bragging, and combative. He
once had tried to prepare for the priesthood, for which "he demonstrated no vocation." Worst of all, he scandalized everyone
by attempting to sell and franchise a liqueur called "Salette," a
project which was broadly considered as profiteering from the
apparition of the Holy Mother. He died when he was forty.

After she had learned to read and write, Melanie tried unsuccessfully to live within a number of religious orders, including a Carmelite convent in Darlington, England. As the years passed, it is said that she was difficult to get along with and increasingly became opinionated, obnoxious, and eccentric. One source indicates that she was bitter regarding the clergy for their failure to proclaim her personal importance.

Eventually she called herself "Sister Mary of the Cross, Victim of Jesus" — "Victim of Jesus" referring to the church, not the Savior. She died alone in 1904 while dressing for Mass, which she had attended daily ever since seeing Our Lady of La Salette.

4

Lourdes, France

(1858)

By 1858 the reputation of the great apparition at La Salette was twelve years along, and Emperor Napoleon III had been in power for ten years. Even though he exercised direct dictatorial power and no one dared go against his will, to the surprise of many he was proving to be an inspiring force.

Under his management, France underwent rapid material progress. Railway building was encouraged, and rail networks for the first time began uniting the nation into an interconnected whole. Cities were rebuilt. Paris was redesigned by the emperor himself, and its now familiar wide boulevards and spacious parks were constructed under his direction. Napoleon authorized the first investment banks, the construction boom gave jobs to thousands, and the economy improved. Napoleon's foreign ventures were also successful at first, and the Second Empire seemed on its way.

Catherine Labouré had not yet died, and her complete story was not yet in the open. The reputation of La Salette seemed secure, and no one imagined that another apparition, even greater than the one at La Salette, would soon occur. The French were therefore astonished when, during February 1858, electrifying rumors began spreading that the Holy Mother was back again, and once more at a place few had heard of.

Lourdes is situated in the Bigorre region of southwest France on the northern slopes of the Pyrenees, the formidable mountain chain between France and Spain. The French side of the Pyrenees receives abundant rainfall and has always been famed for its beautiful scenery, rushing torrents called *gaves,* and abundant mineral waters. Many of the mineral springs had long been turned into fashionable spas at which the wealthy congregated, bringing money and employment. Yet poverty, even appalling poverty, was still everywhere.

The small town of Lourdes did not have a mineral spring and therefore was deprived of any hope of economic benefits. Even so, it seems to have been an idyllic town on the Gave de Pau joined by the Lapacca Torrent, on the opposite side of which were the hospital and school of the Sisters of Nevers.

On the frigid winter day of February 11, 1858, three young girls bundled in poor garments went outside of town and over a bridge to a rocky promontory at that time surrounded on all sides by the icy waters of the Gave de Pau.

They went there to search for sticks or brushwood to burn and discarded bones to cook into soup, although the area had already been picked clean by others before them. All three were suffering from severe malnutrition.

At the farthest west end of the promontory, but back across the smaller expanse of water, was a towering rock cliff called Massabielle. Into the rock was a quite large hollowed-out area, referred to as a cave or grotto, before which grew some brush and a nearly dead wild rose bush. The older girl went there to search for some sticks.

When the two other girls went to look for her, they saw her kneeling down before the cave, her face turned upward. They ran to her thinking she was injured. Instead they found her transfixed, her eyes dilated, and they were unable to move her arms. They started screaming in fear.

The transfixed girl was Bernadette Soubirous, in two weeks to become arguably the greatest seer ever — while the simple cave was to become the greatest and most majestic grotto in history. In twelve days the poor town of Lourdes, population less than three hundred, was to find itself stampeded by over twenty thousand pilgrims, and by fifty thousand more one month later.

The early years of Bernarde-Marie Soubirous, known to history simply as "Bernadette," comprise a tale of appalling and excruciating poverty. She was born on January 7, 1844, the first of eight children of François and Louise Soubirous, in the Boly mill, where her father worked and in which the family lived.

When she was eight her father lost the sight of his left eye in an accident at the mill. Two years later, when Bernadette was ten, he was fired from the mill, from which the family was turned out, forcing them to live in increasingly impoverished circumstances.

The growing Soubirous family was helped out by a distant relative, one Sajous, a stonemason. He allowed them a ground-floor unit, a "stone cage sweating with damp," called "the dungeon" because it had once been the town's prison.

In 1855, a cholera epidemic broke out in the Bigorre region of the Pyrenees, and Bernadette was taken ill. Many died, but she recovered, although for the rest of her life she suffered from severe asthma. Famine also accompanied the epidemic. For a day's food the family often had to share one loaf or less of bread, or no bread, and a watery soup sometimes stewed from bones picked in the streets or from the surrounding countryside. François Soubirous, clearly desperate, was arrested for theft, but the charges were dropped.

The household now began suffering from such grim privation that the fireplace was perpetually unlit. Jean-Marie, the family's eldest boy, was caught going into the local church to eat the soft wax from the candles there and was threatened with jail by the prelate. By February 1858 the family was starving. Bernadette, often coughing and gasping for air, was fourteen. She could neither read nor write.

The apparition to Bernadette Soubirous is particularly well documented, indeed overdocumented — which means there are many versions. Four versions, each slightly different in small details, were written by Bernadette herself, the first in 1861, after she had learned to read and write.

In her own words what Bernadette first saw was a "soft glow" about midway up in the cave which she had seen on two earlier scavenging trips. This time a "beautiful girl" appeared within the soft glow. When the beautiful girl beckoned to Bernadette, she "was frightened and didn't respond." However, all the sources agree that her two companions found her kneeling in a trance-like state. The two girls were one of Bernadette's sisters and a mischief-maker named Jeanne Abadie. The two girls managed to shake Bernadette out of her fixated state, and she told them what she had seen.

On the way home, Bernadette apparently met another sister and again recounted seeing the beautiful girl within the soft glow. The sister told their mother. Jeanne Abadie ran through the town with the gossip that Bernadette had seen a vision and was crazy. Various ladies of the town then came to inquire of her mother. Her mother was upset by the stories, and her father also became upset. Bernadette was forbidden to go to Massabielle again. And as a warning precaution, perhaps as a demonstration to the curious women, both girls "were beaten" by the mother for "telling lies." The following evening, though, Bernadette mentioned the matter to the priest at confession and asked him to tell Father Peyramale, the parish priest. Father Peyramale showed no interest.

By Sunday, February 14, somehow Bernadette had achieved her father's permission to visit Massabielle again with the first two girls. Seven more went along with them. But this time they went along equipped with holy water. Bernadette knelt before the cave, prayed, and shortly again saw *"Aquero"* — meaning "that one" in the local Bigourdan patois. This time she sprinkled holy water on the Lady, which apparently caused *Aquero* to smile.

At this point, Jeanne Abadie, who had climbed atop Massabielle over the cave, rolled a large rock down which crashed near Bernadette. By then, though, Bernadette had become frozen on her knees in an "entranced state" and no longer responded to her companions' cries.

The inability of the girls to awaken her caused them to panic. Two or more ran back to town, where they found the help of a local miller who returned with them and carried the oblivious Bernadette, "smiling at something no one else could see," back to his mill, where she slowly recovered.

Meanwhile, Jeanne Abadie again gossiped all over town. Bernadette's mother was now terribly upset and worried about her daughter's sanity. The predominant feeling in the town was one of disapproval, and on Monday after school, Bernadette was jeered and mocked in the street and slapped by a woman she didn't know for "putting on comedies."

But a prosperous woman, who sometimes hired her mother as a servant, intervened and under her influence it was arranged to take Bernadette back to the cave early the next day, Tuesday, February 16. This time Bernadette was provided pen and paper and would ask *Aquero* to write her own name down.

Early on Tuesday, Bernadette visited the cave for the third time, but now accompanied by a much larger group of silent people who jostled for vantage points on the edge of the river in front of the rock of Massabielle. Some of these witnesses carried rosaries, probably to ward off evil.

Bernadette knelt and assumed "ecstasy." No one besides Bernadette saw anything, but in spite of that two adults nearby asked her to be sure to get *Aquero*'s name. In her ecstasy, Bernadette asked them to be quiet. After a time, Bernadette came out of her ecstasy, not having obtained the name.

When asked why, Bernadette said: "I did ask her. But she said it is not necessary." After some silence, punctuated by some grumbling from the gathered witnesses, Bernadette said: "But she asked me, 'Will you have the goodness to come here for fifteen days? I don't promise to make you happy in this world, but in the next.' "

The nameless apparition had spoken! And spoken of this world *and the next!* Thus began what is sometimes referred to as the "fortnight of apparitions" which were either fifteen or sixteen in number depending on which source is consulted. It is certain that the next apparition was the fourth one.

And it is also certain that when Bernadette again approached the cave, she was accompanied by a hundred or more people. As news of the apparition spread about, the whole population of Lourdes became interested, with a considerable "draw" from surrounding villages.

By the mid-point of this fortnight, the assembling crowd had grown to more than eight thousand, and at one point the crush was of such a magnitude that Bernadette had to be escorted by armed soldiers to the cave — by then and forevermore to be called "The Grotto."

Interrogations of seers are part of the dramatic action of the apparitions, but those regarding Bernadette are so well recorded at length that I'll review them only briefly here.

One of the principal facts is that the cantonal vicar of Lourdes, Abbé Peyramale (described as austere, severe, and inflexible), remained aloof from the situation. He referred to Bernadette with "the deepest suspicion" and possibly encouraged the police to threaten her with prison for causing public disorder.

Thus, Bernadette's first inquisitors were the local police. After either the fourth or sixth apparition, Police Commissioner Jacomet ordered her brought directly to his house in the center of town. Most reports state that he found her modest, sincere, not grasping for money or attention, but otherwise "incomprehensible."

Sources provide different versions of the Jacomet interview, but these are largely contrived, since no one was present to write it down directly. It is agreed, though, that either in the first interview, or in the second interrogation, Commissioner Jacomet finally "lost his temper." He subjected her to "humiliating outrage" and finally prohibited the young seer from visiting Massabielle again with the threat of prison if she did.

However, the second Jacomet interrogation came to an abrupt

end because of "angry crowds" gathering outside that apparently could hear Jacomet's shouting and began hooting and demanding the release of the seer.

The next day, Bernadette "ignored the prohibition" and, accompanied by an even larger crowd, went again to Massabielle. But the apparition didn't appear. At the same time, the mayor of Lourdes defied the police prohibition when he realized the growing strength of public opinion in the seer's favor and when arguments also arose. In any event, at the sixth day into the apparition sequence, the town's civil authorities found themselves solely preoccupied with crowd control matters as pilgrims began pouring in.

After the ninth completely stunning apparition (to be described below), Bernadette was again summoned for interrogation, this time by the town's imperial prosecutor, a more serious business. But this interview didn't go very well, apparently because once confronted with Bernadette's "incomprehensible" answers and statements the prosecutor lost the threads of his arguments and became "flustered."

Again the now vastly enlarged crowds outside demanded the release of the seer and furthermore jeered and ridiculed the prosecutor by broadly gossiping that he was afflicted by St. Vitus Dance (a trembling disease) and that the candles in his house had "lit up by themselves" while Bernadette was there. Shaken, the imperial prosecutor gladly released the child.

Subsequently, Bernadette was again summoned, this time by the examining magistrate and the regional commandant of constabulary from Tarbes, a nearby town. However, it seems that the central topic of this interview was not Bernadette herself or the nature of the apparition, but how to control the crowds which by now had begun to inundate the entire area around Lourdes and Tarbes.

The distance Father Peyramale had engineered between the apparitions and the church began narrowing as a result of the thirteenth apparition (on March 2) in which *Aquero* asked Bernadette to "tell the priests" that people were to come to the grotto in procession and that a chapel was to be built there. This was electrifying news in a situation that already had become highly charged.

To deliver this message, Bernadette, accompanied by two aunts, her mother's sisters, and a crowd of approximately two thousand ambling along behind, went to Father Peyramale's residence.

Father Peyramale did not like this delegation of three, because he apparently had once expelled the two aunts from the Children of Mary School after both had become pregnant before marriage. His anger so confused and intimidated Bernadette that she and the aunts left his presence before she remembered to give him *Aquero*'s requests.

It was then decided to have a friendly sacristan brave the priest's wrath, and when the sacristan finally presented the Lady's requests to the priest, Father Peyramale was confronted with having to make decisions on behalf of the church.

Father Peyramale demanded that *Aquero* should give her name. Some sources state that he also demanded that she should cause the nearly dead rose bush at the front of the grotto to bloom at once in the wintry cold. Other sources omit reference to the rose bush or state that it didn't exist in the first place. The existence of the rose bush was probably factual, since mention of it is included in the early reports Jeanne Abadie spread through the town (that the Lady appeared above and to the side of it.)

After the fifteenth apparition, however, it is almost certain that no evidence of it could be found — largely because anything that could be taken as a souvenir had been snatched up by many of the eight thousand wanting a devotional memento. If the bush had bloomed, it would be certain that its flowers would have been snatched as relics, then its stalks and stems and even the roots.

Father Peyramale's request for the name was put to *Aquero* during the fifteenth apparition. Again the name was not forthcoming. It's entirely likely, as many claimed, that Father Peyramale now smiled to himself regarding this anti-climax. In any event, he now considered that no church decisions regarding the apparition were needed and that Bernadette was at an end.

And, indeed, even though Bernadette returned to Massabielle daily the apparitions of the fortnight period now appeared to cease — to the great disappointment of the growing crowds. However, the dramatic action at Lourdes was by no means over with and indeed had just begun.

Popular opinion among the crowds had already decided that the identity of *Aquero* was that of the Blessed Virgin Mary. Bernadette had begun saying the rosary while kneeling at the grotto and said that *Aquero* asked for "Prayer for sinners." Who else could *Aquero* be than the Holy Mother?

Many in the attending crowds claimed they saw the Blessed Virgin at the site and "heard voices" from nowhere, and several children went into fits, ecstasy, or hysterics. By the fifteenth apparition, and in spite of the clergy's objections, the site had become utterly packed with votive images of the Virgin. Believers in the apparition were at that time still called "cultists" having "simple souls" (read "stupid souls"), and these numbered significantly among the crowds.

The cultists had lit vast numbers of candles at the site and left them burning, which the police of Lourdes and Tarbes considered a fire hazard. Even so, the environs of Massabielle "glowed very beautifully at night." Many had tossed money into the cave since there was yet no one in particular to receive it. Thus, the situation had begun to move out of the control of the town's officials and local clerics and pass directly into the hands of popular devotion. Among the arriving crowds were increasing numbers of educated and skeptical people (as distinguished from illiterate peasants and "ignorant believers"). The apparition was not being taken lightly.

But the apparition at Massabielle might have faded into history were it not for the critical ninth apparition during the fortnight period. The ninth apparition took place either on Thursday, February 25, or Friday the 26th. During that apparition, Bernadette unexpectedly arose from her kneeling position, but not from her ecstasy. She first turned away from the cave to face the Gave de Pau. A hush fell over the crowds, numbering at this point about three thousand.

She was seen momentarily to look back at the apparition, which no one else could see, as if asking for instruction. She then shook her head in some kind of assent. She began to move again, but this time toward the cave, then slightly into it. She knelt at a dry spot — and feverishly began digging with her hands.

Almost immediately some muddy water welled up in the shallow depression she had hollowed out. She drank some of this, washed her face with it, and plucked and ate some grass along the edges of the muddy hole. She stood and walked out of the cave with her face covered with mud and still chewing the grass. Some of the observers nearby started giggling, and others hooted that she had finally gone mad. Pandemonium ensued, with shouts to "Arrest her!"

Bernadette had to be escorted to a house on the rue des Petites-Fosses in town. It wasn't until reaching this safe-house that Bernadette said that *Aquero* had directed her to dig at the dry spot and to "drink and wash yourself at the spring and eat the green you will find growing there."

Later that afternoon, people arriving at Massabielle saw a new stream of water pouring down from the rock grotto and flowing into the Gave. Indeed, the flow increased as they watched. By the next day the spring was producing about twenty-five thousand gallons of clear, fresh water every twenty-four hours.

There was living in Lourdes a "simple quarryman," one Louis Bourriette. According to medical confirmation, he suffered from incurable amaurosis (he was going blind). Louis Bourriette asked that some of the spring water be brought to him. He bathed his blinded eyes with this water — and could see again, a fact confirmed by the town's doctor.

Early the next day this electrifying news inspired a woman, Jeanne Crassus, suffering for ten years from full paralysis of one of her hands, to go to Massabielle. There she dipped her crippled hand into the water for a few moments, and when she again held it up for all to see it had returned to a functional normal hand.

The news of these miracles spread like wildfire. A "roar of acclaim" began among the thousands of witnesses grouped at Massabielle. The ruckus soon spread into the town itself, where church bells began ringing. People were milling and shouting and sobbing in the streets, and the "commotion could be heard at some distance into the countryside."

There were riots at the cave as thousands tried to get at the water. More cures instantly took place. Police, now accompanied by soldiers, arrived to try to restore order. They were overcome by the crowds, and anyway most of them joined the masses attempting to drink the water.

It's quite difficult to comprehend how Abbé Peyramale and his canonical associates, the Fathers Pomian, Serre, and Pene, could have remained aloof from these cures. Yet they did, condemning them as "nonsense," and were assailed for this "stern viewpoint." The first cures, however, caused Father Peyramale to concede that Bernadette "must be honest" after all. But there was yet no theological issue involved, and the clerics remained uninterested.

But during the sixteenth apparition, on March 25, the feast of the Annunciation, an unavoidable religious issue entered into the dramatic events. On the morning of that day, Bernadette awoke very early with a "strong desire" to revisit the grotto. Her parents made her wait until 5:00 a.m., at which time she went along with her family and a large group following her. Bernadette had been to Massabielle daily since the last of the fortnight appearances, but during what is called the "three-week lull" the apparition had not appeared. This time *Aquero* did.

Although recorded details differ as to why, this time it seems that Bernadette was determined to find out who the Lady was. She put the following question three times to her. "Mademoiselle, would you be so kind as to tell me who you are, if you please?" *Aquero* began laughing. But when Bernadette repeated the question the fourth time, the Lady stopped laughing, smiled, and said in Bigourdan patois the thunderous words: *"Que soy era Immaculada Councepciou."*

At this, Bernadette immediately stood up and, with a large train of anxious people following her, hastily went into town repeating the words out loud again and again in order to remember them. Once in town she and a wide-eyed group burst into Father Peyramale's house. Bernadette looked up at him, he down at her, and she simply said: "I am the Immaculate Conception."

Father Peyramale was shocked, for here not only was there a religious issue, but a significant one, and it was one which he knew that the illiterate Bernadette could know nothing about.

This is a complicated, even a bitter issue. Since from at least the fourteenth century the dogma of the Immaculate Conception of the Blessed Virgin Mary had been a source of controversy. It was accepted that Jesus had been immaculately conceived, that is, from the moment of his conception he was sinless. The question was whether Mary herself had been immaculately conceived.

The Lady had finally identified herself as the "Immaculate Conception" — which meant that she was, indeed, the Blessed Virgin Mary, Mother of the Savior, and Mother of the Holy Roman Catholic Church as well. There is no doubt that Bernadette understood nothing of this since its meaning had to be explained to her again and again — and she never fully understood its implications until after she entered the local hospice of the Sisters of Nevers, where she learned to read and write.

For some weeks the grotto had been barricaded by the frazzled authorities, not so much to discourage devotion, but to contain the sewage and public health problems brought about by thousands of visitors. An outbreak of cholera was a major concern.

No one really knew what to do about the site, and vigorous battles between the local authorities and cultists began raging

about what should be permitted there. As soon as the spring began flowing and cures were reported, local craftsmen had devised
a tank to contain the water equipped with outlet pipes, and a
board for holding candles.

Crevices were designed in the grotto into which money could
be inserted, then gathered and delivered — to the formerly reluctant Father Peyramale. Rosaries were said every day, and over
fifty people had claimed to have seen the Virgin. As the cultists
got out of hand, in early May the prefect of Tarbes threatened
to arrest anyone "seeing visions" and incarcerate them. The police commissioner at Lourdes confiscated all devotional objects,
and in June the grotto was boarded up, although the walls were
pulled down several times by energetic cultists.

As these difficulties were proceeding unresolved, news of the
appearance of the Blessed Virgin and the miraculous water had
been circulated throughout France.

The difficulties were finally resolved by a chance occurrence.
In mid-August, the imperial family was in summer residence at
Biarritz, only some ninety miles from Lourdes. There the prince
imperial, son of Emperor Napoleon III, then two years old, had
"contracted dangerous sunstroke and the threat of meningitis
from it."

The emperor, or more probably the empress, sent the imperial
infant's governess to Lourdes, where she first interviewed Father
Peyramale and then Bernadette. The governess then went to the
grotto and in the emperor's name ordered the guards to fill a large
bottle with water from as near the center of the spring as possible.
This the guards scrambled to do. The royal infant was sprinkled
several times with the water. He promptly recovered.

In October, Emperor Napoleon III, in gratitude, personally ordered the officials of Tarbes and Lourdes to permanently remove
the barricades from around the grotto — which was more than a
hint not to interfere with public access to it.

In November a commission of inquiry was appointed by the
bishop of Tarbes, whose hearings took four years to complete.
In addition to the theological issues involved, the commission
doubtlessly considered the emperor's decisive interest, the abun-

dant offerings, and the growing sales of devotional images. The bishop's commission "from the first was deeply impressed" by Bernadette's sincerity and by her "authority and clarity of mind."

In 1862, Monseigneur Laurence, bishop of Tarbes published the expected conclusion:

> *We judge that Mary Immaculate, Mother of God, really appeared to Bernadette Soubirous on 11 February 1858, and on subsequent days, eighteen times in all. The faithful are justified in believing this to be certain. We authorize the cult of Our lady of the Grotto of Lourdes in our diocese . . . [and] in conformity with the wishes of the Blessed Virgin, expressed more than once in the course of the apparitions, we propose to build a shrine on the land of the Grotto, which has now been acquired by the Bishop of Tarbes.*

The bishop's document also proclaimed seven of the cures that had taken place in 1858 to be miraculous. Media response, already great, now became enormous.

In 1862, Achille Fould, a Jewish financier and former French minister of finance, purchased an estate near Lourdes which he intended to develop. He quickly convinced the Southern Railway Company to extend through Lourdes and his estate the railway under construction from Tarbes to Pau.

In this way, the poor citizens of Lourdes found themselves directly linked by rail to the rest of the continent — and linked to sources of income forevermore. Organized pilgrimages could now arrive by train, which they did in increasing numbers and have done ever since, and these pilgrims required hotels and restaurants and other amenities.

In this way did the greatest healing shrine in European history arise. Thousands of cures have taken place there, although only sixty-four had been officially recognized as of 1970.

While the commission was studying the matter in July 1860, Abbé Peyramale and the mayor of Lourdes prevailed upon the mother superior of the hospital and school of the Sisters of Nevers to take Bernadette in as a boarder.

She was sixteen and still "as ignorant as a baby in the cradle." She thus left her family in some grief — a very proud family which, ill provided as they were, refused to accept any form of assistance, except for the healthier house arranged for them by the Abbé.

At the hospice Bernadette had to see many visitors, for inquiries and investigations were going on. The sisters were amazed by her humility and her strength during fatiguing interviews. This seer behaved as a proper vehicle of the Holy Mother should.

She increasingly suffered from asthma attacks, and in the spring of 1862 her lungs became inflamed. As Extreme Unction was being performed she opened her eyes, demanded water from the spring, drank it — and was cured.

She was later transferred to the motherhouse of the order at Nevers over three hundred miles to the north of Lourdes where, as Sister Marie-Bernard, she remained in humility and obscurity until her death on April 16, 1879, at thirty-two years of age. In the same year, Napoleon's only son, the former prince imperial, nicknamed "Loulou," was speared to death fighting for British interests in the Zulu wars in Africa. He was twenty-one years of age.

Bernadette's body was exhumed for the first time on September 22, 1909. It was found incorrupt, and the process of beatification began. It was again exhumed on April 3, 1919, forty years after her death, and found in the same incorrupt condition — except for slight discolorations of the face which were corrected with preserving wax.

The body was then placed in a glass coffin and for many years could be viewed by the faithful and sightseers in the chapel of the motherhouse at Nevers. In 1933, she was canonized as St. Bernadette.

In 1906, the grotto and basilica were confiscated from the bishopric of Tarbes by the French state, and in 1910 ownership of it was transferred to the municipality of Lourdes. The first papal visit to the shrine of the apparition of Our Lady of the Grotto at Lourdes took place in 1982.

The most famous healing shrine in the world, long since a vast and splendid place, is annually visited by over fifteen million people.

5

Pontmain, France

(1871)

As of 1859, France had experienced a beneficent watershed of no less than three glorious apparitions of the Holy Mother — and even Emperor Napoleon III had positively intervened in one of them. The "dry period" was definitely over, and many of the devout began wondering when yet another appearance would occur, for it was beginning to seem that France was favored by the Holy Mother and by God.

Meanwhile, in the political arena after 1859, new problems began to appear under Napoleon's rule. To be sure, and much to the surprise of his enemies, Napoleon III had gained enormous political and popular support. Economic growth for the nation was fostered, and the laboring classes were content with many reforms. Suppression of his opposition took care of the rest.

To satisfy the demand for new Napoleonic glory, however, it was necessary that the Second French Empire have a vigorous and successful foreign policy. The Crimean War gave the French some transient glory, but without lasting results. In spite of the emperor's best efforts, various political snarls and entanglements followed. Napoleon's effort to win a place against Prussia, France's traditional enemy, grew complicated.

Prussia itself had designs of empire in Europe and already had united itself and the German States under the German Emperor William I. This unification was viewed with apprehension by the

French, for the Prussians had already occupied Austria in 1866. There was little doubt that the Prussians would soon turn their attention toward France.

Prussia also possessed a true military genius, Otto von Bismarck, who skillfully manipulated Napoleon's political failures in order to bring about the Franco-Prussian War. Sentiments became increasingly inflamed, and on July 19, 1870, Napoleon fell into Bismarck's trap and declared war on Prussia-Germany. Napoleon then took active command and marched his armies to the German-French border.

Now, as many feared, Napoleon's estimation of his own military prowess failed. On August 4 the Prussian armies crossed the French border, dealt the French a staggering defeat, and captured the French emperor. When this news reached Paris, panic ensued and chains of command rapidly broke down — but not before Napoleon's enemies at the capital seized the opportunity to depose him *in absentia*.

The Prussian armies then moved toward Paris, and by October the beautiful French capital was surrounded and under siege. Other contingents of the Prussian armies kept moving westward from Paris, burning and pillaging along the way.

By January 16, 1871, the Prussians had arrived in Brittany, about 150 miles west of Paris. Nine miles ahead of them was the small town of Laval with the hamlet of Pontmain nearby. Everyone in the area was in panic, and the roads were loaded with refugees trying to escape the advancing onslaught. The population of Laval at the time was about five hundred, and that of Pontmain about one hundred or two hundred, depending on which source is consulted.

Thirty-eight young men from Pontmain had been conscripted into the French army, and everyone was worried whether they would make it back. Among these was August Friteau. On January 17, 1871, the village undertaker, Janette (or Jeanne or Jeannette) Detais, learned that he was safe. Later in the "evening" (about 5:45 p.m.), Mlle. Detais went to the farm of Friteau's stepfather,

Cesar Barbadette, to pass on the good news to him and his family, since they had not heard from August for over three weeks.

She found Cesar in his barn in the pale light of a resin candle working with his two young sons after their evening classes. The three were breaking down furze (a spiny evergreen shrub) to make it edible for their horses. The Barbadette barn was quite large, stuccoed, with a large green doorway. Snow had fallen in the morning, but now the night air was clear and cold.

Eugène Barbadette was twelve, and Joseph was ten. Eugène was August Friteau's half-brother and was fond of him. Although the elder Barbadette and Joseph stopped furzing to listen to Janette's good news, inexplicably Eugène instead went to the open door of the barn and began gazing out.

He is reported later to have said that he went out to look at the sky and at the stars just beginning to appear. But when he noticed "a lack of stars" over a nearby house, he stood gazing and wondering why. The house in question, according to an existing photograph, was across the road, inside a stone fence and wooden gate, and belonged to Augustine Guidecoq. As Eugène studied the starless void, "suddenly" he saw a "tall beautiful lady" about twenty feet above the center of the Guidecoq house's roof.

Eugène insisted that he first thought this was the announcement of his half-brother's death (apparently he had not listened at all to the conversation in the barn). However, he then changed his mind for the "lady was smiling."

He called to Janette Detais to look at the Guidecoq house and see if anything was there. Janette responded that she could see nothing. Cesar Barbadette and Joseph came to the barn door, but the father could see nothing. Eugène asked Joseph if he could "see it." Whereupon Joseph immediately stated that there was a "tall beautiful lady" in the sky above the roof.

The two young boys excitedly began describing to each other what they were seeing. Cesar and Janette continued looking in vain, and soon the father told the boys that there could be nothing there because if there were then he and Janette should be able to see it too.

The various versions of this story now become confused. But it appears that Cesar asked Janette not to mention this because of possible "scandal." Janette willingly agreed not to, and she left. Cesar and the boys went back to pounding the furze. But in a few moments Cesar asked Eugène to go and see if he could still see "it," and after he looked again his answer was "Yes, she's still there."

Cesar's wife, Victoria, at work preparing supper, was now brought out from the Barbadette house without being told anything. When she was asked, she said she could see nothing either. But Joseph was clapping his hands at the "beauty of the lady" — for which his mother slapped him on the arm or head and ordered him to be silent because "everybody is looking at us."

Whether a group of people had gathered by now is not clear. But at some point, the cries of the two boys had been heard by the neighbors, who must have been curious. Victoria ordered her sons to recite five Hail Marys, after which she asked the boys to look again.

They insisted they could still see the apparition, so Victoria went to get her glasses to see if they would help her see something. Still she could not see anything, and she ordered everyone into the house to eat supper. It was about 6:15 p.m.; all the events up to this point had taken place quite quickly.

The boys went unwillingly, their eyes still fixed to the place above the Guidecoq house. After dinner (and apparently another five Hail Marys), the two dashed outside to find the "beautiful lady" still silently in existence. After a few moments of looking, they ran back inside and said that the woman was still there and that "she was about the same size as Sister Vitaline." Barbadette and his wife sent for Sister Vitaline, who was "found in her classroom reciting her office."

When Sister Vitaline arrived at the Barbadette's, she too could see nothing. She promptly left, accompanied by Victoria, who begged her to say nothing about all this. But once back with Victoria in her building, Sister Vitaline found Françoise Richer, eleven, and Jeanne-Marie Lebosse, nine, sitting near the kitchen stove keeping warm. Sister Vitaline apparently decided to take these two girls to the Barbadette farm without telling them why.

Once there, and still separate from the two boys, the two girls immediately spotted the apparition. And both simultaneously described it as a "tall beautiful Lady with a beautiful blue dress with golden stars" — as the two boys had already said.

At this point, a Sister Marie-Edouard had arrived. Sister Marie-Edouard could see nothing; but she indicated that if the children could "see," then other youngsters should be sent for.

Sister Marie-Edouard ran to the house of a M. Friteau (not the father of Eugène and Joseph) and asked him to bring his grandson, Eugène Friteau. Eugène Friteau apparently saw something, too, but for reasons not given he is not considered one of the "principal seers."

When it was found that the other children could also see the apparition, Sister Marie-Edouard then ran to the nearby rectory. "In a trembling voice" she asked the pastor, elderly and infirm, to come quickly to the Barbadette place, where she is reported to have said, "There is a wonder, an apparition! The children see the Blessed Virgin!"

The descriptions of the Virgin at La Salette and at Lourdes had circulated throughout France. But the Lady at La Salette was dressed in yellow, while Bernadette had briefly described the Lady as simply dressed in a white gown and pale blue sash with golden roses on her shoes. This Lady, however, was dressed in dark blue, which didn't even match the standard versions of the Holy Mother.

In any event, Sister Marie-Edouard rushed ahead of the elderly priest back to the Barbadette house where, for reasons unexplained, she knelt and began singing the "Rosary of the Japanese Martyrs."

Meanwhile, at the Barbadette barn, the wife of Boitin the bootmaker, had arrived with her little daughter, Augustine Boitin, two years old, who pointed excitedly at the sky figure, exclaiming, "The Jesus, the Jesus!"

A crowd of some fifty people had gathered, and the pastor finally arrived to ask the children what they saw. They described the apparition again, as they had already been asked to do by other new arrivals. But now they were reporting some changes, since referred to as its "phases."

Some arguments ensued, and a Jean Guidecoq in particular is reported as demanding of Eugène why the boy should see the apparition when he couldn't.

By now the group had gotten larger. Some were singing and others were on their knees — at which point it appears that Joseph Babin, a Pontmain resident, arrived to cry out, "The Prussians are at Laval! We have to pray!"

Meanwhile, the apparition was taking on another phase. Letters of the alphabet were beginning to form around the apparition, and as they did each of the seer children screamed them out in unison. About a hundred townspeople had now arrived, sixty of whom had crowded into the barn trying to keep warm. But the seers seemed oblivious to the cold. Each time the "beautiful Lady" smiled or laughed (apparently many times), the children enthusiastically reported it nearly in unison.

Sister Marie-Edouard and/or Sister Vitaline were now leading the crowd in singing the hymns "Inviolata" and the "Magnificat." When the hymns were finished, the crowd knelt in silence, broken only by the joyous exclamations of the young seers who kept reporting the emergence of new phases and of new letters around the apparition.

Now, while the crowd was silently praying, Sister Marie-Edouard sang the hymn "Ave, Maria Stella" during which the apparition underwent more changes. Not long after the hymn was finished, the apparition slowly began disappearing from the feet upward until, at about 9:00 p.m., the children said, "It is gone."

News of the event spread "like lightning" throughout the parish, in which "not a single incredulous person" could be found.

The next day refugees in flight from the Prussians, people from Laval and from surrounding villages, arrived to pray outside of the Barbadette house, or in the barn where it was warmer.

The earliest written account of the apparition was published by one Father Richard and translated into English by August 5, 1871. This effort appears to provide the basis for all subsequent versions, while later modern accounts are very brief. No really grueling investigations, typical of many other apparitions, seem to have taken place. The difficulties of war probably explain why the apparition was not investigated in greater detail.

It was immediately and generally accepted that this apparition was a prophecy signalling that the invading Prussians would not reach Pontmain, that Pontmain was protected by the Holy Mother, and that the war would promptly end. The reasons are found in the several "phases" which this nonspeaking apparition underwent.

Eugène Barbadette, who eventually became a priest, later provided a description of what he saw. His description, which has been accepted as the principal one, has been translated several times, and possibly revised. In the following account I have reorganized it slightly.

According to Eugène's statements at the time, at first there was an area over the Guidecoq house that didn't have stars; as he wondered about this, the apparition apparently just burst into view. The woman was of extraordinary beauty, appearing to be about eighteen and tall of stature. (She was also described as the size of Sister Vitaline, whose measurements have not been recorded.)

The smiling Lady wore a long garment of deep blue which was covered with five-pointed gold stars, all of the same size and brilliance, but not emitting rays. The stars were not very numerous and seemed to be scattered throughout the folds of the garment.

The deep blue garment was "ample," with strongly marked folds, and fell from neck to feet without "any kind of girdle or compression at the waist." The sleeves also were "ample" and fell over the hands. On the feet were *chaussons* (slippers) of the same blue as the dress and ornamented with gold bows.

On the head was a black veil, half covering the forehead, concealing the hair and ears and falling down to and in back of the shoulders. On the head, on top of the black veil, was a gold crown "resembling a diadem," higher in front and widening out at the sides. A "red line" (or band) from "five to six millimeters wide" horizontally encircled the crown at about the middle.

The hands were small, the face was slightly oval, and "smiles of ineffable sweetness played about her mouth." The head was not bent either to the left or right.

This description is in agreement with the other young seers' accounts of what happened during and immediately after the apparition. This description also constitutes the first of the five identified "phases." Apparently the apparition remained this way for about two hours as a static tableau with little or no motion, except for the smiles of ineffable sweetness.

Different sources describe the phases differently, and so it's difficult to know in what order they took place. But just after Sister Marie-Edouard had recited the Rosary of the Japanese Martyrs (even then an obscure rosary) and just after the priest had arrived, the apparition suddenly began changing into its second phase.

A small "red cross" appeared on the left side of the robe where the "heart would be." Then a "blue oval frame" appeared around the Lady, containing on its inside four unlit candles. Then the figure and frame "grew" until the figure inside achieved about twelve feet in height.

The stars of the sky outside of the oval then appeared to move and "form in order" before the Lady by arranging themselves "two by two" beneath the feet "like people standing on each side when a carriage is passing by." At the same time the gold stars on her robe increased in number.

When Sister Marie-Edouard started singing the "Magnificat," the third phase commenced. The Lady raised its hands until the palms faced outward just above her shoulders, this taken as a sign of blessing and protection from the Prussians.

A large white "surface," about a yard and a half broad and

about twelve yards long, appeared below the Lady's feet and the blue oval. It seemed to the children as if an "invisible hand was slowly forming beautiful letters in gold" upon this "tablet or paper."

For some reason, unexplained, the "Magnificat" was interrupted, and during the temporary silence letters of the alphabet began forming on the "paper." The first one was "M," and the children shouted it out in unison, as they subsequently did as each letter appeared. Finally the French word *Mais* ("But") was formed. Sister Marie-Edouard resumed singing the "Magnificat."

The Lady was smiling again, and the children reported this "with squeals of joy." Slowly thereafter, the first sentence was complete. *"Mais priez mes enfants"* ("But pray my children").

While these words were slowly being printed out, as it were, the fourth phase began. The small red cross over the Lady's heart grew into a larger one now held on the chest by the hands. A new sentence was soon completed: *"Dieu vous exaucera en peu de temps"* ("God will soon answer your prayers.")

When the children had conveyed these words, everyone gathered understood that they referred to the course of the war, and many "joyfully" whispered or shouted that it would soon cease. At these hopeful shouts the children giggled and said the Lady was laughing too.

As if confirming this, and as the fifth phase commenced, the last of the words were printed out: *"Mon Fils se laisse toucher"* ("My Son allows Himself to be moved"). Simultaneously, the red cross disappeared, the Lady held out her hands, and a "star moved around within the frame" and lit up the candles clinging to the inside of the blue oval — after which the moving star came to rest above the Lady's head and crown. (Some versions have it that an image of Christ, red in color, appeared on the red cross before it vanished.) After the candles were lit, the Lady lowered her hands and two small white crosses "were planted on the shoulders of the Blessed Virgin."

At this point, the children began reporting that "a great white veil is rising from beneath her feet." This rose slowly upward, covering the Lady to the waist and then slowly higher until only the face remained smiling down on the seers. It too, and the blue oval, disappeared, leaving only the stars around the crown and the four candles burning. Then these too vanished.

The children grew silent. The pastor asked: "Do you still see?" The seers replied, "No, Father, all has disappeared. It is over."

Although some skeptical criticism must surely have existed, I've not been able to find a trace of it regarding this apparition. And it appears not to have been rigorously investigated, although clerics clearly would have compared their opinions.

One factor, though, has been challenged — and usually relegated to hearsay. News of this apparition of the Holy Mother had "shot through the countryside," and before the next day was over it had spread into Paris itself and, before three days were over, throughout France. It is historical fact that the German army halted its advance on Laval at about 5:30 p.m. on January 17 as the apparition was beginning. It is claimed that General Schmidt, the Prussian commander, was heard to say, "We cannot go farther. Yonder, in the direction of Brittany, there is an invisible Madonna barring the way."

The Prussians halted their terrible onslaught and never reached Pontmain, only five miles away. On January 18, the German forces began retreating from Laval until they arrived back at Vaiges twelve miles away.

Almost immediately the next morning, pilgrims began arriving in increasing numbers to pray. At some point soon thereafter the Barbadette barn was converted into a shrine and a mural of the Guidecoq house and the apparition was painted inside. All who talked with the children were "struck by their sincerity and candor." Whether or not this was an apparition of the Holy Mother seems never to have been an issue.

Four years later in his mandate of February 2, 1875, the then Bishop Wicart of Laval said:

We judge that the Immaculate Mary, Mother of God, has truly appeared on January 17, 1871, to Eugène Barbadette,

Joseph Barbadette, Françoise Richer, and Jeanne-Marie Le-
bosse, in the hamlet of Pontmain. We submit in all humility
and obedience this judgment to the supreme judgment of the
Apostolic Holy See, Center of Unity and infallible organ of
truth in the entire church.

The building of the basilica on the site of the apparition had
already been commenced three years earlier, in 1872. The Barbadette barn, the Guidecoq house, and the local church were
pulled down to make way, and the new basilica's splendid Gothic
towers eventually rose above the rolling countryside of Pontmain.

The basilica was consecrated on October 15, 1900. In front is a
plaza in which there stands a statue of the Lady, which is thought
to be the spot where the Guidecoq house stood.

At some point during the 1950s or 1960s, a towering sister
basilica was dedicated to Our Lady of Pontmain, Mother of Hope
and Peace, in Vietnam, just before the hideous conflicts there.

The German Empire of William I did not occupy France, largely
because England and Spain objected and diplomatically threatened war. Instead, the French agreed to pay indemnity of $1 bil-
lion (a considerable amount back then even for a government),
which was paid off in three years. Some thirty years of French
prosperity followed, which lasted until 1914 and the onset of the
World War I.

6

Knock, Ireland
(1879)

The holy event at Knock is important in the history of the Holy Mother's apparitions because it is the first in the modern period to have *group witnesses* of the apparition itself. The seers of the four combined French apparitions total at most only ten individuals, one at Paris in 1830, two at La Salette in 1846, one at Lourdes in 1859, and either four or six at Pontmain in 1871.

Technically speaking, "seers" of an apparition usually fall into some kind of trance-ecstasy state, although the six young seers at Pontmain did not do so. "Witnesses" can observe phenomena such as miraculous cures, springs bubbling up, predictions coming true, and other astonishing phenomena. "Group witnesses," however, all see the apparition and without falling into ecstasy. Indeed, just about anyone who happens to be in the area of the apparition usually sees it.

In the past, skeptics have dismissed witnesses and group witnesses as suffering from "mass hallucination" and have usually refused to consider their testimony.

As mentioned above, the many photographs taken in 1968 at Zeitoun, Egypt, call for an energetic, positive reassessment of "mass hallucination" regarding the apparitions of the Holy Mother.

Prior to 1879, the Irish had endured unfortunate circumstances, political, economic, religious, and otherwise. Major among these plights had been the severe potato famines from 1840 to 1851. These famines could have been alleviated by the English, who had plenty of food but refused to help, resulting in untold misery. The famines resulted in over one million dead and caused the emigration of many more than that. As a result a deep core of hatred and mistrust for the English has continued until today.

Severe discrimination obtained between the upper and lower classes, between the landlords and workers, between Catholics, Protestants, and Anglicans, between the Irish and the English. Enormous gulfs existed between the wealthy and the poor — the latter very numerous both in the manufacturing centers and on the farms.

These problems had deep traditional and seemingly unyielding roots. Major questions were home rule, representation in the English Parliament, and a more equitable distribution of lands to ordinary people, lands held by the wealthy and by the Irish Anglican Church.

The disestablishment of the Irish Anglican Church brought about by William Gladstone, the British prime minister, caused great commotion in England and Ireland. But it made new lands available, and in 1870 the first Land Act to favor the tenants was passed.

The act made it more difficult for landlords to evict tenants or to treat them as slaves and gave the tenants some compensation for their improvements. The act also aided some tenants in becoming proprietors of their own land. However, no protection was provided against unjust rent increases nor was relief given to tenants whose rents were in arrears. Suffering among the poor, especially among the Catholic poor, was severe.

"Knock" is a derivation of the Gaelic *Cnoc* (hill). Knock, Ireland, sits atop a small hill looking out over otherwise expansive boglands, upon which the larger town of Tuam is located some distance away. On a clear day Lake Corrib can be seen to the west and beyond that the Twelve Pins mountains, over which rain-storms from the Atlantic Ocean sweep inland across the County Connemara.

At the time of its holy apparition, Knock was described as a small hamlet "remote, uninteresting, and undistinguished," or, to put it more bluntly, poverty-ridden, ugly, and boring.

The chapel at Knock had been built in 1829 when Irish Catholics had obtained some measure of freedom to practice their religion. Thereafter the little church served as the focal point of the united parishes of Knock and Aghamore within the bishopric of Tuam.

But the Great Potato Famine had blighted the area, and Knock slowly began to devolve into a place of forgotten fields and forlorn farmhouses. The hamlet itself consisted of only a dozen humble homes. In 1879 no less than eighteen families had recently been evicted in Knock and the surrounding area, and it seems there was little reason for the hamlet to continue existing in its misery and desolation.

On August 21, 1879, most of Knock's few inhabitants spent the day making hay, bringing home turf from the bogs to burn and cook with, or stacking wood in preparation for the coming cold of winter. During the afternoon, thick clouds blew in from the Atlantic, shrouding everything in mist and heavy drizzle. By seven in the evening there was heavy and continuous downpour.

Archdeacon Cavanaugh had been visiting parishioners during the day and had arrived drenched at the hamlet's presbytery. His young housekeeper, Mary McLoughlin, had a turf fire going, where he dried himself and prepared for an evening in.

At about 8:30 p.m., the housekeeper left the presbytery to visit a friend, Margaret Beirne. As she walked in the downpour past the church she noticed some "beautiful strange figures and an altar" standing outside the church's south gable. Although she saw "a white light" around the figures, she supposed that the archdeacon had ordered "the statues" from Dublin and had left them standing out in the rain. Thinking nothing more about it, she continued on her way to Margaret Beirne's house.

However, Mary McLoughlin was not the first to see the "beautiful figures." It turned out that a Mrs. Carty had seen them, too, and, thinking of how they would be paid for, said to herself, "Another collection, God help us."

Margaret Beirne's daughter, Mary, had also seen the figures, or "something luminous," when she had gone at about 7:30 to lock up the church, but she hadn't mentioned anything when she got home. Mary McLoughlin and the two Beirne women gossiped until the former decided to return to the presbytery, and young Mary Beirne decided to accompany her part of the way.

When they again passed by the church, it seems that the "something luminous" was now even more luminous. Both the girls could see that the figures seemed to be "standing on top of the grass blades" but that their "feet didn't touch them." They also observed that the downpour had not wet the south gable of the church and that the grass and ground beneath the figures were dry. Some sources indicate that the two girls immediately identified the three figures as St. Joseph and St. John with "Our Lady" in the middle. This seems unlikely, although it is quite probable that the central figure was "recognized" as the Holy Mother.

The two girls were "astonished," and Mary Beirne excitedly ran back home to tell her mother, also named Mary Beirne; her sister, Catherine Beirne; a niece, Catherine Murray, aged eight; and Mary's brother, Dominick. Mary Beirne excitedly told them all to run to the church because the "Blessed Virgin is there."

Dominick told her not to make a fool of herself. But Mary paid him no attention and rushed again outside to alert the neighbors. Dominick Beirne suggested that his mother go fetch her back before "she makes a show of herself before all the neighbors."

Mary Beirne (locally referred to as the "Widow Beirne" to distinguish her among the town's many other female Beirnes) arrived at the church soaked by the downpour and also saw the figures, as well as the intensely luminous light.

Shortly afterward the Widow Beirne, Mary Beirne, and Mary McLoughlin were joined by Dominick and Catherine Murray, as well as a number of neighbors. All of these also immediately witnessed the apparition.

Young Catherine Murray went flying to fetch an Aunt Margaret, who came along with neighbors, other Beirnes included. It is not improbable that all the inhabitants of the small hamlet came to see, including the archdeacon; but accounts differ as to how many gathered and are consistent only in establishing that all who came to see at this point actually did witness the apparition.

Of the witnesses formally interviewed, fourteen gave direct evidence before the diocesan commission which examined the matter two months later. These witnesses ranged in age from six to seventy-five. Among them were a number of members of the extensive Beirne family — which enabled critics to suspect "family collusion" or "family hallucinating" as an explanation for the "alleged apparition."

Some accounts state that more than two hundred had gathered in the rain, that most fell down upon their knees upon seeing the apparition, and that many refused to be interviewed for fear of being thought irrational or mad. At the inquiry several additional people came forward stating that they had seen from a distance and through the rain a "great light covering the whole gable of the church" and had wondered what was happening there. Some of these had rushed to the church to find out and witnessed the sight also.

What the witnesses saw, however, is difficult to decide. All saw the apparition, but some saw more than others. According to Widow Beirne's formal statement, which is generally representative of most of the others:

I went out immediately and came to the spot indicated. When I arrived there I saw distinctly the three figures. I went in immediately to kiss, as I thought, the feet of the Blessed Virgin; but felt nothing in my embrace but the wall [behind], and I wondered why I could not feel with my hands the figures which I had plainly and distinctly seen.

From the statement of Bridget Trench, seventy-five at the time:

The three figures appeared motionless, statue-like; they were standing by the gable of the church [which was] in the background, and seemed raised about two feet above the ground. The Blessed Virgin was in the center; she was clothed in white, and covered in what appeared to be one white garment.

Her hands were raised to the same position as that in which a priest holds his hands when praying at Holy Mass. I remarked [remembered] distinctly the lower portions of her feet, and [tried] to kiss them three times; she had on her head something resembling a crown, and her eyes were turned up heavenward.

It was raining very heavily at the time, but no rain fell where the figures were. I felt the ground carefully with my hands, and it was perfectly dry. The wind was blowing from the south, right against the gable of the chapel, but no rain fell on that portion of the gable or chapel in which the figures were. There was no movement or active sign of life about the figures.

The statement of young Mary Beirne:

[The figure] of the Blessed Virgin was life-size, the others apparently either not so big or not so high as her figure; they stood a little distance out from the gable wall, and as well as I could judge, a foot and a half or two from the ground.

The Virgin stood erect, with eyes raised to heaven, her hands elevated to the shoulders or a little higher, the palms inclined slightly toward the shoulders or bosom; she wore a large cloak of a white color, hanging in full folds and somewhat loosely around her shoulders and fastened to the neck; she wore a crown on the head — a rather large crown — and it appeared to be somewhat yellower than the dress or robes worn by Our Blessed Lady.

In the figure of St. Joseph, the head was slightly bent, and inclined toward the Blessed Virgin, as if paying her respect; it represented the saint somewhat aged with gray whiskers and grayish hair. The third figure appeared to be that of St. John the Evangelist; I do not know, only I thought so, except the fact that at one time I saw a statue [of that saint] at the chapel of Lekanvey, near Westport, County Mayo, very much resembling the figure which now stood before me.

Above the altar, and resting on it, was a lamb, standing with face toward St. John, thus fronting the western sky. I saw no cross or crucifix. On the body of the lamb and around it, I saw golden stars, or small brilliant lights, glittering like jets [beads] or glass balls, reflecting the light of some [other] luminous body.

I remained [watching the apparition] from a quarter past eight to half past nine o'clock. At the time it was raining.

One boy said he saw angels "hovering during the whole time, for an hour and a half or longer; I saw their wings fluttering, but not their heads or faces which were not turned to me." The "angels" were thus facing the altar, too, as were all the witnesses. Another small boy, John Curry, saw "two angels flying back and forth."

Some of the witnesses noted carvings of "saints and angels" on the altar's lower portion, while some saw a cross behind the lamb. Some saw "lights," or only lights, not the figures, and one saw a "halo of stars."

All of the official and unofficial witnesses, however, agreed that there was a brilliant or luminous light just in front of the church's south gable wall, consistently described as one that "shone like silver" — a cool white light. All of those who could see the figures stated they were bathed in this light.

The apparition apparently lasted until about 11:00 p.m., at which time it "faded out." The rain-drenched people began going home. Apparently some people went home earlier because they were drenched, and some went to get dry clothes and came back.

There were at least *three* subsequent repetitions of the apparition. The first occurred the next year on January 2, 1880, and was seen by the Archdeacon Cavanaugh in the presence of at least twenty other witnesses. Again on the night of January 5, 1880, the apparition was seen by a large gathering, including two officers of the Royal Irish Constabulary posted at Knock to keep order among the arriving pilgrims.

Again on the night of January 6, the same apparition was seen by an even larger crowd, including three men from the neighboring town of Claremorris, who stated they were the first to happen upon it.

Throughout these events, unusual "glowing balls" or "circles" of light were frequently reported at the church, at other places in the vicinity of Knock, or in the nearby countryside — most of which were by critics attributed to "bog gas."

Most of the accounts of the events at Knock completely evade the issue of the miraculous cures. The first of these, or at least the first to find its way into a record, occurred eighteen months after the first apparition when a woman, twenty-eight, who had been deaf since the age of six, regained full hearing while visiting the chapel.

Michael Ansborough and John McKenna, both blind for ten years or so, completely recovered their eyesight. Mary Prendergast, unable to walk for many years and carried to the south gable in a chair, walked away unaided.

To date, well over three hundred miraculous cures have been reported at Knock, but have not been treated with the same kind of examination and expert testimony as those which have occurred at Lourdes.

Official veneration for this apparition developed slowly, largely because local church authorities at first tried to discourage it. The first secular press reports did not surface until about four months later, although the news of it had begun traveling "through the Catholic world" almost immediately.

The day after the first apparition, pilgrims began visiting the church, kneeling before the south gable. Not long after the first media reports had circulated in Ireland and England, and then in France, "hardly a bed or chair could be found in Knock to sleep in."

Indeed, it's reported that "the fee to sleep in the hardest chair" in nearby hamlets was "one shilling and sixpence," a large sum of money in 1879. The local economy of Knock improved for several decades thereafter.

Two official commissions were established, the first by Archbishop John McHale of Tuam at the end of September 1879, but he never permitted a statement to be made.

The second formal inquiry was conducted *fifty-seven* years later in 1936, although the need to have this late inquiry is not clear. By the time of the second inquiry, only two of the witnesses were alive — Mary Beirne O'Connell and Patrick Beirne — and so the official versions of what happened at Knock were not augmented much.

Critics of this apparition state that the investigating committees were "too sympathetic to the apparition at Knock" and that "aggressive investigation" was not undertaken. The devout and the curious, however, have cared little about this skeptical nitpicking — especially after additional cures were reported and thousands of pilgrims began visiting the small chapel annually.

Today, the small church at Knock remains an important pilgrimage shrine. A few years ago a new airport was constructed outside of Knock to handle the traffic. The south gable of the church is enclosed in glass.

When Pope John Paul II traveled to Ireland, the pontiff went far out of his way to visit the chapel at Knock. The visit of a pope to any apparitional site is automatically taken as complete approbation.

Many shrines have been erected elsewhere to venerate this holy apparition. The first American shrine honoring Our Lady of Knock was erected at St. Patrick's Church in Newton, Massachusetts in 1950. The Newton church was presented with the original of the famous Currier and Ives illustration of the apparition of Our Lady of Knock.

Almost immediately after the apparition in 1879, another dangerous famine developed and continued to threaten for the next few years. But by this time thousands of pilgrims had visited Knock from other countries and had been shocked by the deplorable quality of life of the Irish poor.

Because Our Lady of Silence, as the apparition at Knock is sometimes referred to, had placed Ireland on the map of human conscience as nothing else might, this time the entire Western world sent food and supplies and the famine was averted.

7

Tilly-sur-Seulles, France
(1896)

Of the apparitions included in this book, the one beginning in 1896 at Tilly-sur-Seulles is the only one to have taken place during an epoch of general calm and prosperity. No one could imagine the enormous horrors soon to come. The Age of Anarchy (1903–1909) followed almost immediately upon this apparition, and then World War I.

The apparition at Tilly-sur-Seulles, however, was exceedingly strange. It got off to a dramatic start and was at first accepted as one of the Holy Mother. But it then evolved in extraordinary ways until it was firmly rejected as a work of the Holy Mother.

It was clearly a sensational event that attracted the analytical capabilities of over two hundred medical and psychological investigators, who, flabbergasted, had to make their way through thousands of observers, pilgrims, and witnesses.

For reasons I'll detail later, however, this apparition should be withdrawn from obscurity and submitted to extensive reevaluation. For in retrospective analysis we can see that it demonstrated an apocalypse-in-action — along the lines of the famous apocalypse narrative given at La Salette in 1846, which *was* accepted as the work of the Holy Mother.

It was an important apparition, directly witnessed at its start by about four hundred people and by hundreds more after that. It is also the first to continue intermittently for several years.

The most complete record of the events is found in the now rare *Historiques des apparitions de Tilly-sur-Seulles* (Factual Accounts of the Apparitions at Tilly-sur-Seulles), a four-hundred-page book published in 1901 by the Marquise de l'Espinasse Langeac. The apparition is now largely forgotten, but any serious student of the apparitions cannot avoid it.

Tilly, as it's called locally, is in the Department of Calvados, about fourteen miles south of the English Channel and the Normandy coastline and about halfway between the larger towns of Bayeux and Caen.

In 1896, Tilly was a small town with a school of some seventy students staffed by three nuns. There was hardly anything notable about Tilly, except that Tilly and its immediate environs had the reputation of having several times earlier been the "scene of epidemics of trances and visions."

Fifty years before (in 1846, the year of the great apparition of the apocalypse at La Salette), there had lived in or near Tilly-sur-Seulles an "extraordinary pseudo-mystic" named Vintras, who had been subject to visions and "so-called supernatural revelations."

It was told that Vintras's visions and revelations had given rise to "consequences as deplorable" as those which followed upon the "imaginings" of Joachim of Fiore in the thirteenth century. What those deplorable consequences were is not clear.

In March 1896, at about four o'clock one afternoon, a young boy glanced out of one of the school's windows opening onto a field to see a "beautiful lady" slowly descending from the sky. As the boy reported this, the other children in the classroom, and the teacher, rushed to the windows and saw the same.

As they watched in what must have been extreme wonderment, it seems that the Lady didn't quite know where to land. After first moving here and there she ultimately came to position herself in the air near a big elm tree across the open field.

The sixty or seventy students and three nuns evacuated the school and raced across the field to see the beautiful Lady closer up. All of them saw the apparition. The beautiful Lady was within an oval-like aura of brilliant greens, reds, pinks, blues, and yellows which emitted "rays." Inside of these rays was the "beautiful Lady." Her dress appears to have been "opulent and Turkish" in style, but it scintillated and changed colors. The Lady stood out in some resplendent and astonishing fashion and was life-size or slightly larger.

Not only had the school's occupants seen the descending apparition, but almost immediately there "was a great concourse of the devout and curious" into the field, all of whom witnessed the resplendent Lady too. Most now knelt in awe and most began praying. The apparition was assumed to be the Holy Mother.

After a short time, the apparition vanished — to return at frequent intervals in the days thereafter, which made the usual conduct of school activities nearly impossible.

The appearances of the beautiful Lady continued sporadically for about four years. They submerged Tilly-sur-Seulles beneath an enormous and continuing press of pilgrims, reporters, the devout and curious, and platoons of religious and skeptical "investigators."

Even on days when the Lady did not appear, crowds of four hundred to two thousand waited anyway. The field and nearby trees became a forest of candles and effigies of the Holy Mother — and a field of sloshy mud as well. When the Lady appeared, the crowds swelled by the thousands. However, this apparition soon began, as it was said, "to surpass comprehension."

Who saw something and who did not is not clear. It is established that all of the students and nuns saw the apparition. It is more or less established that all the inhabitants of Tilly did too, and that at least some of the investigators arriving to debunk the apparition also saw it — which undermined "their convictions." Certain media persons also saw it.

It is also established that fewer people saw it as time passed. Even so, those that could see, most of them adults, described the apparition to devout pilgrims who could see nothing — but "these descriptions were not needed by the great numbers who could see all or portions of it."

A large number of witnesses began describing features accompanying the apparition that others could not see — such as saints, angels, demons, devils, and other assorted edifying or horrible figures — which revolved around the apparition proper in what today might be called "special effects." It was not understood at the time that these swirling figures corresponded to the apocalyptic visions that the two young seers at La Salette had seen in their mind's eye.

The apparition and the accompanying phenomena usually occurred during broad daylight. But the horrible figures were soon thought of as "disquieting" and phantom-like, and some began gossiping about them as being "diabolical" in origin. Whether an apparition was of diabolical or holy origin was, of course, a matter of grave concern.

The "disquieting" phenomena, however, did nothing to reduce interest in the apparition, which continued to recur at frequent intervals. In fact, media reports appear to have increased interest in the happenings — much like the case of horror movies today. So increasing numbers of people were on hand to witness the "ecstasies, trances, fits, and convulsions" which some of the witnesses began to undergo.

It appears that many of the devout or curious simultaneously would go into "ecstasy" or "trance," their eyes fixed on the apparition. They couldn't be jolted by pin pricks, burning candles put to their fingers, or slaps to the face.

During chanting, hymn singing, and praying of Hail Marys and rosaries, some of the seers would fall into states typical of *convulsionnaires* in certain types of religious activity, for example, some Pentecostal ceremonies in the United States, voodoo ceremonies in Africa or the Caribbean islands, or the ecstasies of some at Lourdes (which caused the authorities to board up the grotto and spring there).

The Lady, asking for prayer, spoke through many of those

in ecstasies — as did various angels and demons and phantoms, often in unintelligible languages.

A thirteen-year-old girl, named Jeanne Bellanger, had trances in which her whole body was contorted; while she knelt in ecstasy her spine curved back until her neck touched the heels of her boots. The "sight of this was so painful" that many who looked on it were "positively ill."

Perhaps the most famous of the witness-participants was Louise Polinière, whose ecstasies were "repulsive," but nonetheless achieved for her "a throng of special sympathizers and supporters."

The witnesses Augustine Troplong and Marie Laisne also acquired "enthusiastic supporters" among the crowds coming and going and camping out in the field by the school. Several "male visionaries," all of whom lived in the neighborhood of Tilly, also had enthusiastic followings. But the visions some of these described "were not at all consoling," and sometimes "quite horrible and repulsive." The trances or ecstasies of Marie Martel and Paul Guerard, however, were not considered diabolical, and the faithful supported them enthusiastically.

Some groups supporting the witnesses, composed of a half-dozen to a hundred or more, claimed they saw the same thing at the same time; but other groups say that they saw different things at the same time. Some saw certain "demons," but others saw different ones. Some saw combats "between angels and disgusting creatures."

In short, Tilly-sur-Seulles had experienced yet another "epidemic" of visions and trances. This new epidemic lasted for a little over four years, with the apparitions and accompanying phantoms, angels, and saints gradually decreasing in number and then ending altogether in 1899.

The most important fact of this astonishing apparition, though, is that the original descent from the sky of the beautiful lady was witnessed by at least a hundred people, and that an estimated four hundred to one thousand saw her in her "pristine" state before the complicating epidemic of ecstatics and *convulsionnaires* began.

These dramatic events were almost immediately compared to the sanctity of Lourdes and its seer, Bernadette Soubirous, and the apparitional affair at Tilly didn't measure up. Many miraculous cures were claimed, but these, however interesting, took second place to the more astonishing phenomena. It is understandable, then, why religious officials showed no interest in the apparition, save unofficially to condemn it in the clearest terms.

The events were also popularized by the condemnations of medical doctors and psychiatrists who felt they had a good case of "communicable hysteria" and "mass insanity" to investigate. Thousands rushed from far and wide to observe the crowds.

It should be taken for granted, of course, that a fair amount of deception, fakery, and pseudo-religious posturing became part of the apparitional events. But a broader study of history quickly reveals that the apparition conforms to many notable apocalypse-like past events of this kind. Anyone familiar with apocalyptic visions would instantly recognize the genre in the apparition at Tilly.

The apparition was a version of the holy apocalypse archetype, in which reenactments of heaven *and* hell are demonstrated communally and simultaneously to multiple participants. Such apocalypse-like scenes are recorded in many religious testaments. Many are found in the Bible, especially, but not only, in the Book of Revelation.

Most of the major apparitions of the Holy Mother in fact preceded horrible events soon to come. And indeed, in some of her speaking apparitions the Holy Mother says that she has come to warn — meaning that she comes not merely to gratify placid devotional expectations, but for far more serious matters. She often allows the seers to see depictions of these warnings in their minds.

The term "holy" can refer not only to the spiritually pure, but also to dreadful forewarnings or superhuman and potentially fatal power. Indeed, the most potentially fatal power known is apocalypse, in which the powers of evil and good are in direct combat.

In this sense, then, what happened *after* the apparition at Tilly is directly meaningful to the apparition. Barely fourteen years after the events at Tilly, the north of France, especially the broad area around Tilly-sur-Seulles, was plunged into World War I. The area around Tilly and the Normandy coastline became an apocalyptic wasteland of fighting, trenches, mud, deadly gas weapons, insanity, slime, disease, and death, with thousands of rotting bodies and mass graves. In fact, the spines of dead bodies left unattended for a time will retract causing the head and lower limbs to arch backward until they meet — exactly as happened to many of the *convulsionnaires* during the apparition.

The Great War was referred to as Apocalypse and at the time portrayed as such in the media, poetry, literature, and art. The Great War lasted four years before the enthusiasms of the combatants dwindled from sheer exhaustion — four years, similar to the duration of the apparition at Tilly-sur-Seulles.

I venture these observations because as a long-time student of the paranormal I'm familiar with the nature of omens. Any competent omen-reader would have had no problem interpreting the meaning of the apparition at Tilly-sur-Seulles, for which there are vivid precedents in antiquity and even during the early Christian epoch.

The area around Tilly was also the principal focus of the Normandy landings during World War II, and some of the bitterest battles of the Allied invasion and German resistance took place there. Vast and very sad cemeteries of the two great Apocalyptic Wars are everywhere around Tilly-sur-Seulles.

In retrospect, it is possible to say that the Holy Mother came to warn of the apocalypse just ahead — albeit in a very strange way.

8

Mantara, Lebanon
(1908, 1911)

It is a challenge to summarize the intricate sociopolitical circumstances in Lebanon just prior to the holy apparition there in 1908, the first of the great twentieth-century appearances. The Middle East has a long history of conflicting religions and political powers. Lebanon was part of the Ottoman Empire during the eighteenth century, but England and France had strategic interests there and intervened continuously. Hostility was perpetually present between the various religious communities. The massacres of the Druses in 1860 led to intervention in Lebanon by Napoleon III in 1861. Because of the French intervention, the Ottoman sultan was forced to appoint a French Catholic governor for Lebanon. Since Lebanon was largely non-Catholic, this political-religious arrangement pleased very few, and its negative ramifications were still ongoing in 1908.

The lovely apparition at Mantara took place among the Melchiten, a Christian Coptic sect. "Copt" is a derivative of the Greek word for "Egypt," and the Copts in the Jerusalem area are those Christians who immigrated there from Egypt.

Neither rich nor powerful, the Copts have held their ground in the Holy Sepulchre at Jerusalem with steadfastness in the face of opposition. The main Coptic altar, which backs on to the marble structure enclosing the Tomb of Christ, is firmly enclosed in wrought-iron gates, inside of which glitter candles, lamps, little icons of gold, and a large and magnificent silver icon, brought from Egypt, of Mary with the Holy Child.

In 1908, Mantara was, a small town near Saida, Lebanon, which was still being called Sidon at the time of the apparition. Sidon was a very ancient city, one of the great eastern Mediterranean seaports of the Phoenicians, and was established long before 1400 B.C.E. It is often mentioned in the Bible and was once famous for its beautiful groves of cedar trees (now vanished), vigorous trade, lignite mines, oranges, purple dyes, and glassware. It is thought that glass blowing was invented there in pre-Roman times.

The version of the holy apparition which follows has been reconstructed from various sources, including obscure ones not frequently consulted by other commentators. The version which is probably most accurate is the account of Archimandrite Nicola Halabi from Sidon.

This version was taken down in German in late 1911 by Baroness von Uexkull; from it a literal French translation eventually was prepared. The baroness's version seems reliable and thorough because among other details it lists the names of numerous witnesses.

Mantara, a suburb of Sidon, is on a western foothill of Mt. Lebanon. In 1908 some groupings of poor huts lay between the mountain and the town of Sidon proper. In one of those hamlets (unspecified) there was a Christian Coptic village church with a large grotto nearby. It had been long claimed of this grotto that several apparitions of St. Mary Magdalene had occurred there in the past, as well as some of the Holy Virgin.

These earlier apparitions led to handed-down descriptions that distinguished between the two Ladies — to wit, that St. Mary Magdalene was "beautiful, but not as beautiful as the Holy Virgin." St. Mary Magdalene also "was not as majestic, being smaller than the Holy Virgin, and more blond."

Tradition has it that the apparition of St. Mary Magdalene asked that this grotto "be one of total silence, that no one here partake of food." This was "the Place of Deep Silent Expectancy for those of anxious heart awaiting the return of Jesus Christ."

Thus, it seems that this raw grotto or shallow cave was accepted as a place of silent prayer and often silently visited by the "expectant." This grotto was deeper and larger than the one at Lourdes, and a small chapel with walls and windows had been built inside, but these apparently were in disrepair in 1908.

During the course of 1908, many began reporting that a "glow" had begun to appear at intervals in or near the Mantara grotto — which was taken as indicative of something special about to happen. Because of the reports of the "glows," Archimandrite Nicola Halabi from Sidon began celebrating Masses there.

At this point an altar was set up, first outside the grotto, but then inside. Thereafter two or three small stone-walled rooms (referred to as "the chapel") were repaired. Even though the news of the glowing at the small chapel must have increased temporary interest in the grotto, nearly four years passed before anything happened.

In the early morning of June 11, 1911, Archimandrite Halabi had conducted a morning Mass in the grotto for fifty to sixty people, who were afterward joined by more people. Later, after eating lunch (apparently not remembering the food prohibition of Mary Magdalene), this group then went to the village church about a thousand meters away to attend a small celebration for the resident French viceconsul at Sidon. After this celebration, at about 5:00 p.m., a group of about fifty women returned from the church to the grotto, where they ate supper.

At about 7:00 p.m., seven of the women "approached the grotto" and "were suddenly blinded by a large burst of light that emanated from the altar, which stood [inside the chapel] approximately ten meters from the grotto entrance."

The women first thought that the burst of light was a reflection of the setting sun in back of them. However, the intensity of the light increased and began radiating many wonderful colors.

The women were now not "silent," since their noisy exclamations attracted others near the grotto. More people, estimated at about sixty, then crowded into the grotto and all of them were likewise "blinded by the light."

It would seem, then, that this light was sudden and very intense, and was quickly perceived not to be the sun's reflection. The light seems to have been so strong that no one could look directly into it.

But very shortly it changed into softer "luminous clouds" from which "radiated beautiful and glorious multicolored rays and other shining lights." In the central portion was a woman who was instantly accepted as the Blessed Virgin because she held in her arms "the Christ Child."

There's a bit of a problem concerning the floor plans of the chapel and altar inside the grotto where the apparitional activity was taking place. It is stated that the seven women saw the blinding light when they "approached the grotto," but that the apparition was at the altar which must have been within the two or three small stone rooms built to house it. The records do not indicate whether the first burst of blinding light filled the entire grotto or only came through some doorway or window of the altar rooms.

In any event, the apparition occurred in a room which contained the altar. This was a small room which soon was packed wall-to-wall. Complaints were soon heard from those outside that those inside should exit to make room for others who wanted to see. After some coaxing the altar room's first occupants moved outside so that others could get in to see, and all who got into the room did see the apparition. The number of those who first saw seems to have been about sixty.

Women ran down the hill from the grotto screaming out the news that an apparition of the Virgin Mary was taking place. From there the news was quickly broadcast to the other villages, and soon a "very large number" of people wanted to get into the room to see. Among there were Archimandrite Halabi and quite possibly the resident viceconsul.

The apparition lasted for two to three hours, and everyone who managed to get into the altar saw it, and some for a third and even a fourth time as queues recirculated.

The record given by Baroness von Uexkull gives the names of the first sixty principal witnesses. But at least four hundred arrived and saw the apparition after the news reached Sidon proper, where an account was published in local newspapers.

Lamentably, descriptions of the apparition are not extensive. One question concerns whether the altar was in a small room or not, because according to reports the entire grotto and space around were illuminated by the lights emanating from the apparition. If the apparition was at the altar inside a room, then the illuminations were penetrating the stone and illuminating the entire grotto and beyond. But whether the apparition was inside a room or not, all those rushing toward the grotto could see light emanating from it within a radius of about five hundred feet around the grotto. The illumination is described as pink and blue, slightly undulating, and "penetrated with a brilliant golden and pure white central core." This same "central core" also characterized the apparition of the Virgin who was "bathed in it" together with "a small Christ child."

Both were silent, but both looked out over the assembled crowd, while the Virgin "received all graciously" by nodding her head, "with movements of her eyes and motions of her hands reaching outward," and with "a pleasant smile." Only the upper half of the figures could be seen. This, then, was a kind of tableau which smiled and moved its hands, while at the same time managing to hold the Christ Child.

A visit to the Mantara grotto is sometimes included on the itineraries of those who visit apparitional sites in the Middle East. It was also mentioned in some guide books as late as the early 1950s.

For some years after 1911, large numbers of pilgrims visited the grotto annually. But after the Great War commenced and drew on, this apparition moved into obscurity. Moreover, it was not a Catholic apparition, and so by some Catholics it was considered "anti-pope and outside of grace."

For two years after the beautiful apparition at Mantara — often referred to as the Holy Apparition of Total Silence — the Lebanese of all religious persuasions enjoyed prosperity up until the start of World War I. As the hostilities commenced, however, money and support from abroad ceased, tourism (important to Lebanon) was drastically curtailed, and summer visitors vanished altogether.

Lebanon was then occupied by Turkish troops (under British sponsorship), and local combats took many lives. A long famine ensued, said to have been artificially engineered by the British/Turkish Sandjack command.

9

Fátima, Portugal
(1917)

Portugal occupies about one-sixth of the great Iberian Peninsula, which it shares with Spain. Up until about the turn of the century it had long been an absolute monarchy with extremely close and devout affiliation to the Roman Catholic Church. Some historical sources say that at one time as many as two out of every nine inhabitants were priests or members of religious orders.

Before 1900, anti-monarchy and anti-clerical forces had begun fomenting. By that year, those forces emerged under their motto "The Republic of Terrorists." Vividly put and as cited in contemporary documents now obscure, the rallying cry was to ensure that the "last king would be strangled with the entrails of the last priest."

King Charles I and his son, heir to the throne, were assassinated in 1908 as the extreme revolutionary factions organized to bring about "reform." The next king, Manuel I, wisely fled to England in 1910 and a revolutionary republic was proclaimed. The new republic was headed by a mixture of democrats, socialists, Freethinkers, Marxists, and atheists. The factions squabbled among themselves in order to establish "reform," and the new leaders depended on familiar tactics of ruthlessness and fear.

They regarded the throne, the nobility, and the church as a complex of irrational institutions. It was easy enough to exterminate the royal family lines and to abolish the titles of nobility—

and to open new, and free, universities at Lisbon and Oporto to teach socialism and atheism. But these were ideological matters rather than practical ones. So the leaders of the new republic were soon involved in unfamiliar territory — the tense problems of the working classes, most of whom had worked for the nobility or church and so were now unemployed. The former economic system broke down.

Although the factions squabbled, in one matter all the factions were united. One of the first acts of the new republic in 1910 was to expel all the religious orders and to confiscate their property. This turned into a long, drawn-out affair, for the religious naturally resisted.

Between 1911 and 1916, at least seventeen thousand priests, monks, and nuns were murdered, singly and in groups. Occasionally the entrails and decapitated heads of the murdered were carried in street parades to impress the remaining religious.

This chaotic situation characterized Portugal until 1917. All churches were closed or destroyed. No one dared congregate for Mass or even be seen saying the rosary. Fear ruled — and religion was considered dead. Meanwhile, in 1914, the Great War had begun elsewhere in Europe, the first of the great modern apocalypses.

Then, in 1917, there occurred a great apparition of the Holy Mother — whose images, together with those of her Son, had for seven years been smashed and trampled upon in the streets. The Lady was not happy, and she was now to take extraordinary efforts to impress.

The hamlet of Fátima is located about 110 miles to the north of Lisbon at an elevation of about three thousand feet above sea level. In 1917 it was a poor rocky area inhabited by peasants not many in number. The nearest large town was Leiria, about twelve miles to the northwest, once a famous university and the archdiocesan cathedral, now shut down.

Early in 1916, Lucia dos Santos, age eight, and two younger cousins, Jacinta and Francisco Marto, were tending sheep at

Chousa Velha, a field east of Mount Cabeco, near Fátima. They reported that a "cloud whiter than snow" had formed several times. In this cloud there appeared a youth about fourteen or fifteen years of age, dazzling in splendor. He announced himself: "Do not fear, I am the Angel of Peace. Pray with me."

There are many sources that report the events of Fátima. They are not clear how the news of those first events was treated — but angels, of course, would have been forbidden to appear and would have been dangerous to their seers.

On Sunday, May 13, 1917, the same three children were again tending sheep in a rocky pasture called the Cova da Iria. It was a sunny day. At noon, a beautiful Lady appeared near a shrublike oak tree. According to some sources, she said: "Do not be afraid. I will not harm you." Finding courage to speak, Lucia asked where she was from. "I come from heaven."

Then the Lady made three requests. "I ask you to come here on the thirteenth day of each month, at this same hour, until October. Then I will tell you who I am and what I want." She requested that the children should learn to read and write and that they should "say the beads each day to obtain peace for the world and the end of the war." The Lady parted her hands and a great ray of light streamed from them directly upon the children. Then a "path for her opened in the sky as if heaven were opening up to receive her."

The three young seers, Lucia dos Santos and Jacinta and Francisco Marto, were of humble origin and economic circumstances. Photos show three rather solemn faces, wearing their best clothing, which was plain and common. They could not read or write. How much the seers really understood of the events is open to question. But the messages of the Lady at Fátima clearly went beyond their comprehension — and indeed those messages went beyond the comprehension of most of the world.

Considering the many books written about the events at Fátima, it's surprising to find that descriptions of the Lady are very brief. The earliest reports state that the Lady was a "young

woman of transcendent beauty." She appeared as a radiant, lumi-
nescent form with clearly discernible features in a brilliant aura
which surrounded her and enveloped the children as well.

She seemed to be "composed of the aura" and to have been
transparent. She wore a white garment, with a mantle over her
head. Her hands were pressed together in an attitude of prayer,
and she held a string of pure white beads that ended in a sparkling
white crucifix.

There were six apparitions altogether, each on the thirteenth
of the month, from May 13 to October 13. The third appearance was complex, but through the mouths of the three illiterate
children emerged news and predictions, some hoped for, but
others incomprehensible at the time. The appearance began simply enough. Lucia asked the Lady: "Will you take all three of us
to heaven soon?"

"Yes, I shall soon come to take Jacinta and Francisco. But you
must remain longer here below. Jesus wishes to use you in making
me known and loved. I wish to spread devotion to my Immaculate Heart throughout the world." Many cries were heard while
this somber prediction spread among those gathered. Later Jacinta and Francisco stoically professed themselves unafraid to be
taken to heaven.

Lucia now requested, having been pressed to do so: "I wish to
ask you to tell us who you are, and to perform a miracle so that
everyone will believe that you have appeared to us."

The Lady responded: "Continue to come here every month. In
October I will tell you who I am and what I wish, and will work
a great miracle that everyone will have to believe."

This news was conveyed throughout the crowd. Many fell
to their knees and started praying; others jeered and shouted
"lunatics" and "liars."

But the Lady continued: "Sacrifice yourselves for sinners, and
say many times 'O Jesus, it is for your love, for the conversion of
sinners and in reparation for the sins committed against the Immaculate Heart of Mary.' " As the Lady spoke, she opened her

hands and from them rays of light shone out and "seemed to pierce the very heart of the earth."

The place where earth had been was now a sea of fire. And plunged in this fire were devils and lost souls, as if they were red-hot coals. These floated about in the conflagration, carried about by the flames issuing clouds of dark smoke. Sparks fell in great conflagrations among shrieks and groans of sorrow and despair. The children were so frightened that "they could have died." But the Lady continued:

> *You see Hell — where the souls of poor sinners go. To save them, God wishes to establish in the world the devotion to my Immaculate Heart. If they do what I will tell you, many souls will be saved. And there will be peace.*
>
> *The war [World War I] is going to end. But if they do not stop offending God, another and worse one will begin in the reign of Pius XI.*
>
> *When you shall see a night illuminated by an unknown light, know that it is the great sign that God gives you that He is going to punish the world for its crimes by means of war, by hungers, and by persecution of the church and the Holy Father.*

The Lady then went on to enunciate a prediction which at the time was incomprehensible:

> *To prevent this I come to ask the consecration of Russia to my Immaculate Heart and the Communion of Reparation on the first Sundays. If they listen to my requests, Russia will be converted and there will be peace. If not, she [Russia] will scatter her errors throughout the world, provoking wars and persecutions of the church. The good will by martyred, the Holy Father will have much to suffer, various nations will be annihilated. In the end my Immaculate Heart will triumph. The Holy Father will consecrate Russia to me, and she will be converted and a period of peace will be granted to the world.*

"In Portugal," the Lady said, "the dogma of the Faith will always be kept." The Lady then gave a secret message, the major part of which was not to be released until 1960.

Reports on the events and messages of the third appearance were soon in print, sneeringly so in Portugal's newspapers, and also were conveyed to the world by the Catholic media. As might be imagined in 1917, the concept that the dogma of the faith would always be kept in Portugal utterly outraged the revolutionary authorities, who had control of the media and had already taken extraordinary steps to crush religion there.

Vicious diatribes were published, holding the children and the apparitions up to intense ridicule by publishing every word — with commentary that "the superstitious idiots, desperate to have something to support their unfounded religion, are provoking mass hysteria and hallucination."

Moreover, in July 1917, it seemed that the Great War would never end. The children's message that it would soon end was sneered at. The war ended in November 1918, after German resources were exhausted and morale had collapsed.

Pope Benedict XV was sixty-three at the time and so, it seemed, with a long pontificate still ahead of him. The three young seers' report that the next war would begin during the papacy of a pope named Pius XI was unimaginable by them, and everyone else as well. Benedict XV died in 1922, by which time the messages of the Lady had been broadcast throughout the entire world, including the prediction about Pius XI.

As is well known, popes are elected by secret vote, and immediately upon their election each pope selects the name he wishes to be known by as pope. Achille Cardinal Ratti, born in 1857, just three years after Benedict XV, was elected pope in 1922 — and he selected Pius XI as his name. He still occupied the papal throne in 1939 when, as the Lady had predicted, World War II began.

As for the "unknown light" which would be seen as an omen confirming that another great war was shortly to come, on the night of January 25, 1938, an extraordinary auroral display was seen over Europe, extending as far south as northern Italy, into France, Spain, and Portugal. Such auroras are usually confined to the Arctic circle. World War II began twelve months later.

The Lady's prediction in July 1917 about Russia "spreading its errors throughout the world" and "persecuting the church" was completely unintelligible at the time — and was not to become even partially intelligible until at least a decade later. It is difficult to see how anyone could have invented it.

It was true that Nicholas II had abdicated the Russian throne in February 1917. But a democratic Duma (congress) had been set up, and it was expected that a vital democracy would ensue. Vladimir Ilyich Lenin had earlier been exiled from Russia and did not return until February 1917. He was again forced to flee to Finland in June 1917 and did not return again until October.

Throughout the transition period from monarchy to democracy, there had been a small Bolshevik minority in the first all-Russian Soviet Congress (June 1917). It was not until November 1917 that the Bolshevik minority gained enough power to establish a full Communist government, headed by Lenin, who established the Council of People's Commissars.

As everyone was to discover, Lenin's agenda was to spread his version of Communism throughout the world, preparatory to establishing the first world empire of Communism. But even as late as 1942, it was not clear to the Western world that the Soviets intended to conquer the world.

Between 1917 and 1931, the Russian Communist government carried out a systematic decimation of the Catholic Church. Within a little over thirteen years, 681 parishes and 980 churches were destroyed. Over 1.6 million of the faithful were arrested, deported, or murdered. As of 1954, after the Soviets began annexing other "Soviet bloc" countries, 15,700 priests had been forced to accept other jobs, 8,334 theological seminaries were dissolved, 1,600 monasteries were nationalized, and 31,779 churches were closed.

During the seven years of his dictatorial rule, Lenin was responsible for twenty million deaths. During the following twenty-nine years, Stalin murdered forty-six million. After "Russia's errors" spread to Maoist China, seventy million more would die.

In retrospect, then, it is easy enough to see why, with her foresight, the Holy Mother was worried about Russia — and why she did not like Communism.

Regarding the prediction about the deaths of the two children, Francisco died in April 1919 when he was ten, a victim of the great influenza epidemic that followed the war. His sister Jacinta died in February 1920 from an attack of pleurisy that followed her influenza. She was nine.

At the appointed time of the fourth apparition, August 13, the children were not present. They had been forcibly taken from their families by the local authorities and were being held under threat of imprisonment. But the news of the appearances had gone out. So at the time of the August 13 event, there were about eighteen thousand people congregated in the Cova da Iria area, and they "were impatient." Resentment mounted when it was explained why the young seers were absent.

As the anger and shouts of protest escalated, there occurred a formidable clap of thunder in a cloudless sky. The crowd ran for cover because it was first thought that the authorities had placed bombs at the site. Two earlier shrines, crudely erected at the tree trunk, had already been dynamited by the authorities.

But as the crowd was scrambling, there was a brilliant flash of light over the spot of the apparition — which everyone witnessed, including the spying authorities. The sun now lost its brilliance. The atmosphere became hazy. A small, whitish cloud formed around the trunk of the tree. It was very light, like mist or smoke, golden and very beautiful. It began turning crimson red — then rose, yellow, blue, in rapid succession manifesting all the colors of the rainbow.

The gathered people, as well as the stones and trees, were tinted with these radiating colors. The Cova da Iria became alive with undulating colors. Then the colors disappeared suddenly and abruptly. The sun resumed its usual intensity, and all returned to normal — excepting, of course, the eighteen thousand witnesses, police spies, and few priests on hand (disguised in civilian clothes), all of whom took some time to regain their composure.

Later, on August 19, Lucia, Francisco, and his brother John were tending sheep in a place called Valinhos. When they "felt something supernatural approaching and enveloping" them, they suspected that "Our Lady was about to appear." Jacinta was quickly fetched.

Money had been left by pilgrims at the Cova site, and the Lady instructed that it be used to make two litters, one to be carried by Lucia and Jacinta and two other girls dressed in white, the other to be carried by Francisco and three other boys, for the feast of Our Lady of the Rosary. What was left of the money would help toward the construction of a chapel to be built there.

"We would like to ask you to cure some sick persons," they had asked.

"Yes, I will cure some of them during the year," the Lady responded.

So the litters were built to carry images of Our Lady of the Rosary, and for the first time in seven years religious processions took place. The anti-religious authorities hardly dared to intervene, since several thousand marched in the processions.

The authorities tactfully released their young detainees, so that they could be present at the next event on September 13. The children, along with a crowd numbering about thirty thousand, were present on September 13. According to Lucia:

> *As the hour approached, I set out with Jacinta and Francisco [and their families and a very large crowd], but owing to the crowds we could only advance with difficulty. The roads were packed with people, and everyone wanted to see us and speak to us. There was no human respect whatsoever.... [People] pressed around us...begging us to place their petitions before Our Lady...petitions for cures*

*for sons, husbands, wives, for those gone into the war, for
people suffering from tuberculosis. . . . and so on.*

Again the sun above burned with its usual intensity. The seers
were kneeling, praying, watched by the thirty thousand. Forbidden rosary beads were now in the hands of most attending.
At noon, the sun suddenly dimmed. The atmosphere turned to
the misty, golden tint seen on the earlier occasion. The gathered
masses gazed in silent wonder as the sun grew dimmer, fading
to such a degree that some actually saw the moon and the stars.
Skeptics later tried to convince the world elsewhere that these
phenomena were eclipses, but in fact no eclipses occurred during August and September 1917, as can be confirmed by any
ephemeris.

The thirty thousand witnesses next saw "a globe of light advancing from the east to the west." It traversed over most of
them, past the sight of two watching priests, several media persons, and numerous police observers, and then settled down to
the bottom of the hollow where the children were kneeling.
The tree, first dynamited, then chopped into bits and pieces as
devotional objects, had by now vanished.

As the globe of light came nearer, Lucia suddenly shouted:
"There she is! I see her!" Except for the three young seers, no one
else among the thirty thousand claimed to have seen the Lady,
even though it would have been easy for many to do so. What
the others saw, however, at least those tightly packed around the
children, was that a beautiful, radiant white cloud formed and
encompassed the seers.

This enormous crowd was so tightly packed that no one could
move without hurting themselves. Upon this enormous pack, out
of the cloudless sky above, began falling "shining white globules." Everyone stared upward. The globules grew smaller as they
neared the ground and vanished before they touched it or the
faces of the assembled people. At the time, the globules were
described as rose petals or angels' hair.

The falling globules had their source, visible to all, in a great jet
of light coming down from high above. This vast beam of light

sent down rays that broadened as they approached the amazed throng. The light rays played iridescent rainbows of color over the crowd. At the end of the apparition, the radiant white globe rose up and returned down the valley until it gradually disappeared into the light of the sun, which now returned to its usual brilliance.

News of this event spread throughout Portugal and elsewhere throughout the world. So an even larger crowd was present at the next scheduled apparition, October 13, 1917. Various estimates give the size of this crowd as between seventy and ninety thousand.

During the night of October 12, the remnants of a fearful and unusual storm that had originated in Siberia arrived over Portugal. Blowing westward over Europe, it had scourged with icy downpours both the German and the Allied armies. As the day of the scheduled apparition dawned at Fátima on October 13, the Cova da Iria was bleak. Black clouds scudded from the northeast; shapeless fog, biting and cold, blew this way and that. The rain, pitiless and steady, continued falling.

Photographs exist of the pilgrims gathered to see the Holy Mother's promised miracle. The photos show an enormous sea of big black umbrellas. Early in the morning at least fifty thousand people had gathered, and the number soon increased to between seventy and ninety thousand.

Shortly before noon, the scheduled time, the three young seers arrived. They were escorted by umbrella-carrying members of their extensive families and other close associates. The rain continued as the seers forced their way through the crowd. Every shred of grass and shrubs had been trampled, and beneath the mighty expanse of umbrellas was a vast sea of water and mud. Sanitation was a major problem. The civil authorities were vexed and tired. Antagonistic reporters waited for the miracle they doubted would occur.

The seers were kneeling at the site. Noon passed. Nothing had happened. The enormous crowd grew restless and threatening.

Then the children indicated that the Holy Mother had arrived. Messages were delivered, and the children reported that a tableau of St. Joseph and the Child was being shown to them.

No one else saw anything. Hoots and shouts were heard from among the black umbrellas. The seers said that the Holy Mother was departing. Still no one else saw anything. Shouts of "fraud" and "the children are insane" could be heard. A roar of grumbling built up in the steady downpour.

Suddenly Lucia said the Holy Mother was pointing to the sun behind the roiling clouds. Lucia herself pointed upward. The clouds parted where she was pointing. Lucia shouted: "Look at the sun!" But she hardly needed to tell people to look. As the clouds parted, the sun hung suspended like a great silver disk, and the light hurt no one's eyes. There was a rustle of more than fifty thousand umbrellas being closed. All faces were turned upward, as can be seen in photographs.

As all watched, the sun began rotating, dancing, whirling rapidly like a gigantic pinwheel (the descriptions vary). Then the sun stopped turning. This phenomenon was repeated twice. At the sun's third whirling, there appeared on its rim a border of crimson which flung blood-red streamers of "flame" across the sky, reflecting on the hills, rocks, the upturned faces.

Many screams were heard. A succession of brilliant beams of color radiated from the rim of the whirling sun: green, red, orange, blue, violet, the entire spectrum of the rainbow. The beams themselves were whirling, cascading colored lights everywhere and far toward the horizon. Many had fallen to their knees in prayer.

The sun began wobbling, and then with no warning plunged toward the earth in a zigzag path growing in size as "it came near." Many witnesses were shocked into immobility, but more fell to their knees, fearing instant death, while others scrambled away on the muddy ground.

Then all saw the sun reascend in the same zigzag manner to its usual place overhead. In a few seconds it reassumed its natural brilliance, now hurting the eyes of those trying to look at it. The clouds were gone. It was a brilliant, calm, sunny day.

There was not a drop of water or mud anywhere. In fact there was dust where the mud had been, and the waterlogged shoes and boots and skirts and pants of ninety thousand people were completely dry.

The awe and the silence were profound. Then came the tears and the roars of acclaim. Several skeptical media persons and police were found in weakened, nearly comatose states. It was said that "joy lit up the faces of all" — for the promised miracle had been delivered.

On October 29, 1917, photographs of the upturned faces were published in the Portuguese newspaper *Illustração Portugêsa* and republished throughout the world, along with descriptions of the event. Hundreds of eyewitnesses were interviewed — and most told approximately the same story. A few had seen nothing at all, except that the mud suddenly disappeared and everything instantly and inexplicably became dry.

Skeptics explained that all this was a case of "mass hysteria." But when it was later learned that the phenomena had been seen and recorded by separate groups up to thirty miles distant from Fátima, skeptical criticism dwindled.

After the great event of October 13, 1917, the Portuguese authorities abandoned any attempts to eradicate religion. In spite of some residual opposition, a beautiful statue of Our Lady, carved of Brazilian cedar and painted white and gold, soon was installed in the new chapel at Cova da Iria in May 1920.

In June 1921, Lucia dos Santos entered the Sisters of St. Dorothy at Vilar, where she learned to read and write, and then joined a Carmelite order. For many years no one except the mother superior knew who she was. Even after her identity became known, she continued living in obscurity.

After eight years of investigation, in October 1930 the bishop of Leiria issued a pastoral letter declaring the apparitions worthy of belief and authorized the veneration of Our Lady of the Rosary of Fátima.

The bodies of Francisco and Jacinta were exhumed in 1935.

Quicklime had been poured over their bodies due to the contagious properties of the influenza. Francisco's remains were not found intact, but Jacinta's body was found completely incorrupt, and was again found incorrupt in 1950.

Even during World War II, over five hundred thousand people annually visited the shrine at Fátima. Since then it has been visited by as many as twenty million people each year.

During the Holy Year of 1950, Federico Cardinal Tedeschine, acting as papal legate, celebrated a Solemn Pontifical Mass at the impressive basilica of Our Lady of Fátima standing near the site of the Cova da Iria. Masses were performed at each of fifty-two altars in and around the basilica. Hundreds of thousands received Holy Communion. A special radio broadcast by Pope Pius XII in Rome was heard throughout the world.

And in 1983 Pope John Paul II visited the shrine.

As to the secret message yet to be revealed, Lucia had written it down with instructions that it not be revealed until 1960. Before his death, the bishop of Leiria passed the sealed secret to the cardinal patriarch, who passed it to the Congregation for the Doctrine of the Faith in Rome. It is known that Pope John XXIII read the secret in 1960 but declined to reveal it, presumably because of its apocalyptic contents.

During his visit to Germany in the autumn of 1980, Pope John Paul II was asked by pilgrims about the secret of Fátima. After his visit, his response appeared in the newspaper *Stimme des Glaubens*. According to this report the pope explained:

> *It should have been made public in 1960, but because of its troubling content, and to dissuade the superpowers from undertaking wars, my predecessors in the papal chair have chosen the diplomatic way. All Christians should be content in the knowledge that the oceans will inundate whole continents, and millions of people will die from one moment to the next. Hearing this, people should not long for the rest of the secret.*

Many people would like to know the secret only for sensation. They forget, however, that along with knowledge goes responsibility.... They are not concerned to do anything to avert the impending times of trouble — and this is a dangerous attitude.... Pray, pray — and do not inquire anymore. Everything else should be entrusted to the Holy Mother of God.

10

Beauraing, Belgium
(1932, 1933)

The Kingdom of Belgium had always been a well managed nation. It adopted neutrality in war and experienced rapid industrialization. It early led the continent in the development of railways, coal mining, and engineering. There were, however, political disruptions accompanied by labor unrest and by the rise of the Socialist party in opposition to conservative and clerical groups.

Albert I came to the throne in 1909. Social conditions improved under Albert, but in 1914, in order to attack France by the easiest route, Germany invaded and occupied Belgium, flagrantly disregarding its neutrality. During World War I, the Belgians were subjected to dreadful German atrocities — as they were again to experience during World War II.

The 1932–33 period saw the rise to power of Adolf Hitler. In 1932, Albert I was still on the throne and was fifty-seven. No one ever expects an apparition of the Holy Mother. Even so, the Belgians were surprised to experience not only one, but two in quick succession.

The hamlet of Beauraing was described in 1932 as an "uninteresting place few had ever heard of." It didn't even appear on many maps. Thus those hundreds of thousands hearing of the marvelous apparition had first to find out where Beauraing was, and then "motor there on hardly existing roads, or via horses, carts, or their legs."

However, Beauraing soon appeared on hastily printed maps — thirty miles south of Namur and about six miles east of the French-Belgian border. Beauraing is in the Ardennes region, a plateau traversed by sharp crags, ravines, and wild rivers. It was still very sparsely populated in 1932. At that time the area was suffering from the Depression. The region, especially the Meuse Valley, is a traditional battleground, and the Ardennes saw heavy fighting in both World Wars.

Young Gilberte Voisin's father usually brought her home after convent school shortly after six when his work on the railway allowed. But when he was unavailable, her sister and brother went to collect her, and on November 29, 1932, a Tuesday, these two were also accompanied by the sisters of the Degeimbre family.

The convent school of the Sisters of Christian Doctrine stood on a road on the outskirts of the hamlet and was close up against a railway embankment along which trains puffed their way to and fro. Between the road and the door of the convent was a space "of no great extent," edged by a few ragged trees. In a corner of this space, where a fence separated the convent from the road, had been placed a small shrine of Our Lady of Lourdes containing "a small plaster statue of the type generally familiar." This little shrine was referred to as the "grotto."

It was about 6:30, and already dark, when the four children rang the convent's bell to collect Gilberte Voisin. While the four awaited for the nuns to deliver Gilberte, Albert Voisin chanced to turn his head in the direction of the "grotto" — where he saw "something vaguely luminous" and seems to have been frightened.

The other three children also saw the "radiance," and also were frightened. When Gilberte Voisin came out of the convent, she too saw the luminosity and was frightened as well. Thereupon they "averted their gaze" from the inexplicable "effulgence" and returned to their homes in a "disquieted state." Whether they told anyone of their experience at this point is not clear.

But on Wednesday, and then again on Thursday, coming at the same time to fetch Gilberte, they all had the same experience. Thursday was December 1, and on this date the glad tidings of the luminosity at the small shrine of Our Lady of Lourdes apparently were conveyed to Madame Degeimbre, who was at home with some relatives and neighbors.

Madame Degeimbre and the others set out for the convent to see what all this meant, leaving behind the two younger girls. The Lady again showed herself to the three children, Fernande and Albert Voisin, and Andrée Degeimbre, all of whom fell immediately on their knees and said a Hail Mary.

Madame Degeimbre could see nothing, nor could the other adults. So Madame Degeimbre pushed her way to the grotto — whereupon her daughter Andrée cried out, "Mama! Don't go any further! You're right on top of it!" At this point the apparition seems to have disappeared.

Gilberte Voisin again attended school on Friday, but this time her father went to fetch her himself. At a later hour the five children and a group of adults returned to the shrine, whereupon the five "were simultaneously overwhelmed by the same impression." All five, now in some kind of a "trance" or "ecstasy," fell to their knees and began repeating the Hail Mary aloud — which served "to cause consternation" among the adults.

There are some minor inconsistencies regarding what the apparition looked like. At first it was seen only as a "disquieting luminosity" or "effulgence." But at some point, the children made out a central "luminous human figure." One source says that the figure was three to four feet tall, but this is not included in other sources, although there are references to the "small size" of the central figure. The effulgence was first seen to undulate or fluctuate.

By December 2, the figure had become stationary and recognizable as a "beautiful Lady," and after the Hail Mary was said by the children on that day, Albert Voisin suddenly asked: "Are you really the Immaculate Virgin?" The Lady nodded affirmatively.

Albert then asked: "What do you want us to do?" The diminutive Lady replied: "I want you to be very good."

It appears that the apparition vanished, since it is recorded that the group returned again to the grotto at about nine, but now with more neighbors. On this second visit, the same scene was reenacted, with the exception that it was young Andrée Degeimbre who was asked to be good.

On Sunday, December 4 all five children returned to the grotto — this time with an old man who was blind and a little crippled child about their age. When the apparition appeared, Albert, seemingly the chief spokesperson, asked the Virgin to cure the two. Then, without waiting for the cures and clearly familiar with the scheduled routines during the Lourdes and Fátima apparitions, he asked, "What day shall we come?" To this the Lady replied, "The day of the Immaculate Conception."

At this point, Fernande Voisin, the eldest of the children, asked: "Must we get a chapel built for you?" — whereupon the Lady answered "Yes" and then disappeared. On this occasion, Joseph Degoudenne, a crippled boy, insisted he saw the apparition, too, but upon questioning and comparison it was found that his description did not correspond with those of the five.

On Monday, December 5, the apparition was again seen, but when Albert asked the Lady to work miracles, she ignored him. When he repeated the request, it was again ignored — whereupon the children began to weep. But when Albert asked when they were to come again, the answer was "in the evening."

In the evening, the Lady again showed herself, and twice more on Tuesday, December 6, reiterating the request to come on the feast of the Immaculate Conception, Thursday, December 8, of that same week.

By Tuesday, December 6, Beauraing was only seven days into the apparitions, but by this time a considerable sensation had been caused. Ever larger groups were gathering around the convent to be present when the children came, and newspapers had already sent reporters. The news had begun circulating especially in the Catholic journals of Belgium. The whole nation had soon learned of the apparition, and Belgians far and wide were trying to locate Beauraing on their maps.

By this time the Voisin and Degeimbre families and neighbors and the townspeople of Beauraing were being besieged by interview requests. In press interviews, Fernande and Albert Voisin indicated that the Lady (sometimes referred to as "The Virgin") "was not at all like a grown woman," but only about a meter (about three feet) tall. Her face was young and the dress was luminous and white with bluish tones in it. There was "no blue sash" (typically seen on contemporary statuettes of the Virgin), but her eyes were blue. The hair was hidden by a white veil. The feet were not visible.

By December 8, the feast of the Immaculate Conception, a vast crowd estimated at ten thousand was present. The sources don't describe how the local authorities dealt with this human deluge, their motor cars, and other forms of conveyance necessary to transport such a crowd to Beauraing.

When the apparition appeared to the children on the day of the feast of the Immaculate Conception, they all fell to their knees and into a trance. Several "medical colleagues," present at the request of one Dr. Maistriaux, "physically tested them." Lighted matches were applied to the hands of two of the young seers, all were "pinched vigorously," and one "medical colleague" produced a sharp penknife and applied it with force to their cheeks.

These "tests" produced no reaction of any kind, and when the "affected parts" were examined after the apparition, "not the slightest trace of injury" was found. Later, when "experts more scientific" arrived, they determined that the tests had not been applied effectively enough and that no inference could be drawn from them.

The apparition on the feast of the Immaculate Conception

was little different from those preceding it, except that it came sooner, lasted longer, and was "more brilliant." The principal new features were the now immense crowds and the intervention of doctors. Immediately after this apparition, the children were separated from their parents, taken into the convent, and separately interrogated by doctors, whose cross-examination procedures were "insidiously" repeated on several subsequent days. Two of the experts involved were a Professor De Greeff of Louvain and a Dr. Rouvroy, the head of a psychiatric hospital, whose convoluted reports were promptly published in Belgium and France.

On the four days after the apparition of the feast of the Immaculate Conception, the children attended by still larger crowds went to say the rosary at the grotto, but the apparition did not appear. During the remaining days of December the apparition appeared only infrequently.

On December 17, the children were heard in conversation with the Lady. Speaking apparently in unison, they asked: "At the request of the clergy, we ask you what you want of us?" The children were then heard to say: "Yes, we will have it built here." On December 23, in response to a further question about the new shrine, the Lady replied: "In order that people may gather here in pilgrimage."

The events at Beauraing were attended by at least six thousand people on Christmas Eve. At this time the children made a loud appeal that Our Lady give tangible proof by healing the poor sufferers who were present. This appearance was a short one, and the Lady seemed to be ignoring requests for cures. After this some of the children at times failed to see the apparition, and Albert on at least three occasions "suffered this deprivation." At some point thereafter, the Virgin "intimated that the visions were coming to an end."

On Monday, January 2, 1933, the Lady said, "Tomorrow, I shall say something to each of you in private." The apparition of January 3, 1933, is known as the "Farewell Interview," during which the private messages may have been delivered. Fernande Voisin could not see the first part of the appearance and only heard the word "Adieu," while Gilberte Degeimbre heard "Adieu," and then "I'll convert sinners." Albert Voisin declared that Our Lady had told him something he wasn't to repeat, and he apparently did not, save to say upon questioning "Well, if they want to know, it [the message] was rather gloomy."

To this point, then, this apparition was a weak, diminutive one compared to the sensational ones at Lourdes and Fátima. The hardy Belgians took this in stride and now addressed the question of the shrine that the Lady requested be constructed on the site of the grotto. To build the new shrine required (1) destroying the school and convent of the Sisters of Christian Doctrine, and (2) moving the railroad tracks which ran close to the grotto. An additional complication was that the Belgian clergy were forbidden by higher ecclesiastical authority to organize pilgrimages to the scene. The prohibition was extended to forbid solicitations and contributions for the erection and maintenance of a shrine.

The clergy were also forbidden to permit publication of books, pamphlets, or articles in newspapers, unless these had first been submitted to censorship and received an imprimatur. Belgian newspapers, however, including the Catholic media, had already published frequent and lengthy accounts. The history of the great apparition at Beauraing now seemed at an end, principally because no miracle cures had taken place.

However, in the summer of 1933, there were dramatic new developments. Tilman Come, age fifty-eight, lived in the hamlet of Pontaury, some thirty miles from Beauraing. Described as a "worthy artisan," for six months he had been entirely incapacitated by a disease of the spinal vertebrae diagnosed as spondylitis, which caused acute suffering and which had already brought about an irreversible ankylosis, or stiffening of the joints. He was dying.

Though every movement brought excruciating pain, he managed to convince his wife to have him brought by automobile to

Beauraing. He suffered mightily during the bumpy ride, but arrived in the proximity of the convent on June 11, 1933, where he said a few Hail Marys from inside the car. After waiting a while but feeling no relief, he and his wife resigned themselves to returning to Pontaury.

But at that moment he was seized with spasms of pain so intense that his wife cried out, "He's dying." This attracted a large group of pilgrims who shuddered in horror at his painful twisting. But they were then "astounded and transfixed when Tilman Come stood up erect, got out of the car, and stretched his limbs now perfectly free of pain." Doctors later opined that the seizure was brought about by "some adhesion breaking down."

As the electrifying news of this cure quickly spread into Beauraing proper, everyone fell to their knees, including Tilman Come, and uttered prayers of "heartfelt thanks." But then a very happy Tilman Come explained to bystanders that at the moment of the seizure he had "lost consciousness of things surrounding him" and in a brief trance had clearly seen the Holy Mother, who had "smiled kindly" at him and said that she would "see him tomorrow."

To all appearances, Tilman Come was instantly restored to perfect health. On the trip back to Pontaury, he stopped and heard a late Mass at Hastière and went to a Benediction once back at Pontaury. The next morning he walked three kilometers to Mettet, caught the train to Beauraing to keep his appointment with the Holy Mother, and before an enormous and expectant crowd, was once again favored with an appearance.

But this time he heard the Virgin say: "I have come here for the glory of Belgium and to preserve this land from the invader. You must make haste." This astonishing news implied that Belgium would again be invaded, which seemed very unlikely since Belgium's neutrality was assured by international treaties.

The news of Tilman Come's spectacular cure had energized flagging interest in the apparition, and despite the prohibitions on the clerics news of it was telegraphed everywhere. Four days later

Tilman was back again, this time with the original seers; the five heard the Virgin repeat her request for "a chapel, *a big chapel.*"

Tilman Come now became the principal seer at Beauraing and experienced continuous apparitions until sometime in August 1933. From one of those it was learned that the Lady desired to be called "Our Lady of Beauraing," and a number of "secret" messages were given to him.

The apparition on August 5, 1933 to Tilman Come, now described as a "kindly soul, but very exalted," was attended by a crowd estimated at about two hundred thousand people who had come to "marvel about the demonstration." During this apparition it was discovered that the Holy Mother didn't want the new chapel to be built on the site of the little grotto where she had first revealed herself. This was not to be touched. The new chapel was to be built on the other side of the road away from the railroad tracks — probably much to the relief of the railway authorities. Precise instructions regarding the altar of the new chapel were now described by the Lady; these ultimately were carried out.

Immediately after this apparition, Tilman Come was subjected to a two-hour enquiry conducted by doctors and clergy. From this he emerged "gleamingly unscathed and more exalted to the tumultuous cheers of the 200,000 people." Thereafter, more cures were reported. By late August 1933, some 150,000 visitors *per day* visited Beauraing, and more cures were announced.

But once a temporary shrine was set up, 1.7 million pilgrims visited it during the first ten months (Lourdes at that time was attracting less than a million visitors a year.) It was only a matter of time before the Lady of Beauraing would get the permanent shrine she had requested and personally designed.

In 1935 the Bishop of Namur appointed a commission to investigate the events at Beauraing. He died before the investigation was complete, but it was carried out by his successor, Bishop André Marie Charue.

On February 2, 1943 during World War II and the cruel German occupation of Belgium, the bishop authorized public devotions to Our Lady of Beauraing. This authorization was based in part on two cures accepted as authentic and credited to Our Lady of Beauraing. The miraculous cure of Tilman Come was not one of those.

In another document of July 2, 1949, the bishop instructed the clergy of his diocese to affirm that the "Queen of Heaven" had indeed appeared to the children of Beauraing. This finally permitted official acceptance of contributions in her name, which helped in the construction of the requested shrine, the impressive basilica which was finally consecrated on August 21, 1954.

The first official pilgrimage to Beauraing from the United States arrived in September 1953; at present the shrine is visited by about one million people a year.

All five of the seers eventually married and all had children. The last available report on the whereabouts of Albert said that he was training native teachers in the former Belgian Congo in Africa, now known as Zaire.

11

Banneux, Belgium
(1933)

About fifty-three miles northeast of Beauraing was the tiny and even miserable hamlet of Banneux, about ten miles east of the historical city of Liège. Like Beauraing Banneux appeared on few maps (and even today *The Times Atlas of the World* doesn't identify it). At the time, however, unlike Beauraing, a large part of Banneux's small, nominally Catholic, population favored Marxist socialism and hardly ever had anything to do with the church if they could avoid it.

In what were referred to as the "poorer outskirts" of the already very poor Banneux, Julian Beco, thirty-four, his wife, Louise, and their seven children lived in three small rooms. Julian was an unemployed wiremaker who seldom left the house and was also "a badly lapsed Catholic" who kept his family from church contacts.

Mariette Beco was the eldest daughter, born on the feast of the Annunciation, March 25, 1921, and thus in January 1933 two months shy of her twelfth birthday. She is described as a "truant" from school; not only did she not like school, but she had her hands very full as "deputy mother" for her brothers and sisters and "manager of the family finances."

On the evening of Sunday, January 15, 1933, Mariette was watching through a window for one of her brothers who had gone to a friend's house and was late in returning. It was a moonless night and snowing lightly. As she watched, over a patch of scrub in their little garden she saw a faint luminous figure of what appeared to be a woman leaning her head a little to one side. She told her mother, who first thought that it might be a "witch." Some accounts have it that Louise looked out and also saw a luminous figure of a woman, but in any event Louise did not see the subsequent apparitions.

The apparition disappeared — but not before Mariette had decided it was the Blessed Virgin and was able to give a detailed description of her. She was enveloped in a "great oval light." The gown was dazzlingly white and spotless, chastely closed at the collar, and fell in a "simple dignity" of broad pleats. The sash was of an "unforgettable blue" loosely fashioned around the waist, falling in two streamers at the left knee. A veil of transparent material, but as completely white as the gown, covered the Lady's head and shoulders. The Lady was inclined to the left and slightly forward. The hem of the gown was slightly lifted exposing the right foot "crowned with a golden rose." On her right arm hung a rosary of diamond-like brilliance, whose golden chain and cross reflected the oval aura.

When Julian Beco was told of the apparition, he "was not impressed," and talked about the silly influences of the events at Beauraing. Mariette attended school the next day after being absent several weeks.

There she told a friend about the appearance, and her friend thought the village priest, one Father Jamin, should be told and with Mariette's permission went to tell him. Father Jamin "made light of it" and had no further interest — also thinking it was a "mere echo of Beauraing."

On Monday, January 16, and/or Tuesday, January 17, depending on the source, Mariette went into the garden and again saw the apparition. Much to her father's consternation she was seen kneeling and praying, oblivious to the bitter cold. Some documents have it that it was during the "second vision" that the Lady first spoke. According to others it was the fourth, but in either case it was on Wednesday, January 18, outside of the house in the freezing cold, from which Mariette could not be coaxed into the house.

Mariette's father was "much disturbed in mind" and went to fetch Father Jamin, who was not at home. So he instead asked a neighbor to help persuade Mariette to come indoors. The two, and possibly Louise Beco and the other children, found Mariette walking out of the garden into the road in a trance saying, "She is calling me." The group followed her, lighting the way with a lantern, until Mariette, after kneeling along the way, finally came to a small spring near the road. She plunged her hands into it and then "seemed to come to herself." On being questioned, she stated that the Holy Mother had told her, "This spring is set apart for me" and then said, "Bonsoir, au revoir" (Good evening, good-bye.)

After hearing about these events, Father Jamin came to the Beco house the next day to make inquiries, at which time Julian Beco, to everyone's surprise, asked when he could go to confession, to which he was speedily admitted. After receiving absolution he received communion at the public Mass the following morning, January 20, which made him an object of derision among the Marxist-Socialist constituency of Banneux.

In the garden, when Mariette had asked who she was, the Lady replied: "I am the Blessed Virgin of the Poor." At the spring when Mariette asked the Lady to explain the meaning of the words "this spring is set apart for me," the Holy Mother explained that the spring was "for all nations, for the sick," and that she had "come to bring relief for those who are ill."

On either January 18 or 19, Mariette attended catechism class, "contrary to her wont," which impressed everyone in the hamlet and also gave Father Jamin, now interested, an opportunity to question her and take notes.

In spite of the earlier "good-bye," Mariette knelt nightly in the garden. The apparition reappeared, however, only on February 11, February 15, February 20, and then for the last time on March 2. By now, the apparitions to the children at Beauraing had ceased. On March 2 the Holy Mother gave Mariette one of those irritatingly "secret" messages (never revealed so far as I can discover) and then took final leave with the words: "I am the Mother of the Savior, the Mother of God. Pray much. Good-bye." This farewell apparition took place during a drenching and bitterly cold rain, with hundreds of spectators standing near the Beco shanty.

At some point the spring became "The Fountain," and almost immediately cures were being reported because of its water. By 1934 the water was being bottled and sent all over the world, and Julian Beco had constructed a "primitive little edifice" as a chapel in his garden.

But better buildings were soon being constructed, which threatened "to transform the poverty-stricken character of the scene," as a contemporary media report had it. Like at Beauraing, booths and shanties began lining the roads into Banneux, with religious artifacts for sale. Throngs of pilgrims and visitors descended almost immediately on Banneux although these "were not as large as those at Beauraing." Mariette Beco was packed off to a boarding school to rescue her "from the importunate, if well-meant, solicitations of the pilgrims."

A local committee, including two doctors, two priests, and some of the "more educated residents" quickly investigated "the facts" — and equally quickly and unanimously concluded that no fraud was involved either on the part of Mariette or her family and that Mariette was in good health physically and mentally with nothing to "suggest abnormal tendencies."

Among other details, investigators determined that the phrase "Blessed Virgin of the Poor" could not have been borrowed from any invocation with which Mariette could have been familiar, and indeed that "no such concept had ever arisen within the church."

Furthermore, the phrase "I have come to bring relief to those who are ill" is in French (which the Lady spoke) "Je viens soulager les malades." It was determined that Mariette had never heard the word *soulager* ("to bring relief").

The "case of Banneux" was not resolved by Belgian clergy, but was submitted directly to the Vatican in late 1941 by Bishop Kerkhofs of Liège. The Vatican response was unusually swift, and veneration of the Virgin of the Poor was almost immediately approved and solemnly and officially inaugurated — but with the stipulation that enthusiasm for the apparition should not take precedence over the needs of the poor.

A 250-bed hospital for the poor was quickly built in Banneux, followed by other similar hospitals, staffed by nine religious orders. Five international centers of information on the Virgin of the Poor were set up. Over three hundred chapels, over three thousand monuments and shrines, and twenty-five churches throughout the world were dedicated to the Virgin of the Poor. Over five hundred thousand people a year visit Banneux, and more than fifty miraculous cures had been authenticated by 1953. Mariette Beco eventually married, had children, and relentlessly resisted all publicity.

The apparitions at Beauraing and at Banneux were the last ones to achieve official church approval. The Sacred Congregation of the Holy See at Rome ultimately decided that ecclesiastical approval regarding apparitions was no longer necessary.

During the latter days of World War II, the cruel Battle of the Bulge was fought in the Ardennes, where Beauraing and Banneux are located. This was one of the most deadly, bitter, and costly battles ever staged. It lasted for a month, and cost the lives of 167,000 Allied and German soldiers — over 5,000 dead a day.

12

Kerizinen, France
(1938)

In 1938, few expected another Great War — excepting, perhaps, those who paid attention to the earlier apparitions of the Holy Mother warning of such, and Winston Churchill in England.

Adolf Hitler had been consolidating his power in Germany since 1933, and under Hitler's guidance, Germany had rearmed and become a significant military force. Even by 1936, the handwriting was on the wall, but the world was blind to it. In 1937 Neville Chamberlain became prime minister of England. Like most others, he believed that Hitler was a rational statesman like himself and would not want another war.

The new British prime minister signed a series of "appeasement" treaties with Hitler, culminating in the Munich Pact of early 1938, to which France was made party. Chamberlain said over the radio and to millions of eager listeners who wanted the reassurance that "peace has been achieved in our time." The world was now secure.

In France, a coalition of Socialists, Radical Socialists, and Communists, called the Popular Front, had won the elections of 1936. From then until 1938, the Front enacted important social and labor reforms, before being overturned by conservative opposition, which then assented to the appeasement policies toward Nazi Germany. Far away from these momentous events was Brittany where daily life plodded on no matter what transpired elsewhere.

Kerizinen and Plounevez-Lochrist in Brittany are about three hundred miles west of Paris. Plounevez-Lochrist was a hamlet on Brittany's north coast at the far western end of the country, which juts into the Atlantic Ocean. Kerizinen, about two miles away, was not even a hamlet, but rather a few ancient and poor houses built of rock. About a mile to the north was the seacoast and the English Channel. Everything was usually damp and cold, and storms frequently blew in from the Atlantic.

On September 15, 1938, a sad and lonely woman, Jeanne-Louise Ramonet, was patiently knitting on an embankment while watching over her milk cow grazing in the meadow. It was one of those pale, sunny days typical of Brittany when not obscured by fog and drizzling rain.

A "ball of light" suddenly appeared before her a few feet above the ground. The light expanded and developed a radiant periphery. In the middle of this "globe" there appeared a "young lady of great beauty." Jeanne-Louise fell to her knees and the Lady immediately spoke:

> *Be without fear! I mean you no evil! You will see me [at] different times in the years to come. I shall tell you then who I am and what I want from you. A new war threatens Europe. I shall delay it for some months, because I cannot remain deaf to so many prayers for peace arising toward me at this moment at Lourdes.*

Having said only this much, the Lady "rose slowly, slanting toward the north and disappeared very high in the sky." This incident left Jeanne-Louise stunned, but with the message and the image of the figure firmly etched in her mind. So began the bittersweet apparition at Kerizinen, the first of many to occur intermittently for many decades.

Descriptions of the misfortunes of Jeanne-Louise Ramonet are heartbreaking. She was born in Kerizinen on October 7, 1910

(the feast of the Most Holy Rosary), to Yves Ramonet and Marie-Yvonne Portel. The couple had nine children, four sons and five daughters. The Ramonet farm was one of the smallest in the area. Actually it wasn't even a farm, but rather a small meadow with a small stone house, to which was attached a small stone barn for their two milk cows. The house was about the size of an average kitchen in the United States and was so crowded with beds that there wasn't room for a table.

At the age of two, Jeanne-Louise, described as "small and delicate," was afflicted with paralysis of her right leg, which made walking difficult and thereafter caused her to limp. When she was nine, she suffered painful decalcification of the bones and could hardly go out to school or anywhere else. Her brothers and sisters were healthy. They married and moved away, rather eagerly it seems. Jeanne-Louise didn't find a suitor. After her mother and one younger brother died of typhoid in 1927, and her father in 1930, she remained alone in the small bleak house on the farm.

The family was "solidly Christian," but Jeanne-Louise's education remained "very scanty" due to health difficulties. In 1925, Jeanne-Louise entered the hospital at Brest for treatments for her leg and other health problems, which were not very successful. After this she returned to the farm, where she plodded through her days until 1936, when the parish priest at nearby Plounevez-Lochrist arranged a free trip for her to the healing shrine at Lourdes with a group of sick people going there.

Her trip to Lourdes was unfruitful, and her physical ailments remained unhealed. Jeanne-Louise felt that she had done something to "offend God." But after she returned from Lourdes her health improved until she was strong enough to walk and undertake at least the work of her own upkeep.

For some time, Jeanne-Louise told no one about seeing the apparition, keeping it "secret in her heart." However, the seer later said that she had no doubt that it was the Blessed Virgin and described her as a beautiful young lady, perhaps seventeen years old.

Her dress was a "very sweet" shimmering deep blue, and her eyes were of the same shimmering color. The blue dress was undulating at the bottom and had a white border there, and the sleeves also ended in a white border. A double white ribbon girded the dress at the waist. A shining white mantle, or cape, held at the neck by a golden rectangular hook covered the shoulders and reached down below the knees. A very light, extremely white veil covered her hair. She stood motionless as she spoke, and her head was lightly inclined toward the left side. The arms were positioned as if in prayer, her fingers crossed on her chest. Her left arm was holding a rosary.

Nearly fourteen months passed before the next apparition occurred, on October 7, 1939, the feast of Our Lady of the Holy Rosary and the seer's twenty-ninth birthday. The Lady appeared as before and spoke thus: "The world does not stop offending God with very grievous sins, especially sins of impurity, whence this war as a punishment for so many faults." The word translated as "grievous" was *lourds* in French and more precisely means "stupid" or "thick-headed." The Spanish Civil War had just ended in February 1939, but another war was not yet really in sight, as we shall review below. The Lady continued:

> *But heaven is not insensible to so much misery and comes to give you a means of salvation: peace, you will have it before long, if you know how to acquire it — but for that it is necessary that the people lead a life of prayers, of sacrifices, of penance. It is necessary that very often the children, particularly, be grouped to pray, to recite the rosary, followed by the "Parce Domine" for the sinners.*
>
> *Tell your Director [the village priest?] that he should make public this message. I will give these words a supernatural force that will touch hearts.*

As later documents establish, Jeanne-Louise immediately told the priest about the first two apparitions, as the Holy Mother ordered. But the priest forbid her to say a word about them. So for the next nine years, until after the thirteenth apparition (October 4, 1947), it seems that only the seer and the priest knew about the apparitions — which later gave opponents good grounds for discrediting the first messages when they were finally made public.

An inspection of the Lady's messages shows that the Catholic media, which began presenting the messages after 1947, invariably omitted the last two sentences of the second message, which admonished her "director." The entire thirteenth message is also usually omitted. Among other things, it sternly took the "old priest" to task for failing in his duty to help make the Lady's messages known. Holy apparitions that chastise the clergy are not easily accepted. Jeanne-Louise was often seen limping into the meadow where she knelt and was thought to be praying. Although the Lady had commanded the seer to make the messages known, she did not because her priest forbid her.

If it is true that the first and second messages predicted a war which almost immediately followed, and that subsequent messages accurately predicted the course of France's sufferings, then it seems strange that the priest made no mention of the prophecy. War predictions are not popular. The world was hopefully entranced in visions of "peace achieved in our time," and very few expected another war.

The first message, given on October 7, 1939, refers to "this war [in France] as a punishment." In historical retrospect, the beginning of World War II is dated at September 1, 1939, when Hitler attacked Poland. But hardly anyone realized that this particular aggression would result in universal war, except Winston Churchill, who was ignored.

Britain and France declared war on Germany on September 3, but it was thought that war would be confined to what was needed to reclaim Poland. In fact, the partition of Poland was quickly agreed upon on September 20, and this "False Peace" endured until April 1940. But the Lady's prediction of war in France was given on October 7, 1939.

The false peace ended only when Germany unexpectedly invaded Denmark and Norway on April 6, 1940. Then, in another surprise move, on May 10, 1940, Luxembourg and Belgium were occupied by the Germans. Only on June 10, 1940, after tremendous fighting on French soil, did France sign an armistice which allowed occupation by the Nazis.

In 1938–39 no one in France or Europe, and certainly not in Kerizinen, realized that war on French soil was just ahead. And no one realized that World War II had started before October 7, 1939, when the second message was received nor that France would soon be at war within its own boundaries.

In the third message of December 1, 1939, we find the Lady advising: "Be sure to arm yourselves with prayer and sacrifice while your [French] soldiers are using physical weapons." And in the fifth message of April 2, 1940, we find this warning:

> *The prayers said are less in number than were said in the first months of the war. For this negligence, you [in France] will all go through sufferings, but mainly so your soldiers. Many will be made prisoners and many will die of privations and misery.*

It is almost certain that the clergy did not later invent these messages. Jeanne-Louise was a simple woman, seemingly of very limited intelligence, and remained so all her life. She seems to have been incapable of fraudulent behavior.

In the sixth message, given in early May 1940, when Belgium was just then being overrun, we find: "My children of France, serious hours will soon toll for you! The invasion of your country by the enemy is the danger that threatens you." The gloomy future by then might have been apparent to France's tactical planners. But it is doubtful that this was apparent to Jeanne-Louise or the priests in Kerizinen at the out-of-the-way westernmost point of France.

And what of the prophetic message given in the eighth apparition on May 8, 1941:

Soon Russia will bring help to the war, help which will be a hard blow to your enemies. But, beginning at this time, pray, pray a lot, O Christian souls, for this great enemy of the church — otherwise, after the war, the Communists will be seated nearly everywhere, and the church will receive harassments from them.

This clearly is an extension, or an update, of the warnings the Lady gave at Fátima in 1917. It is quite probable that Jeanne-Louise knew of that message. But how she could or would herself update it is unfathomable.

As historians admit, the meaning of this message could not have been understood or even conceived in 1941. In fact, the Soviet Union was a welcome ally against Hitler's aggressions. The Soviet threat was not to be fully understood until after 1946, and even then only in closeted government circles. Indeed, that the Communists would "be seated nearly everywhere" was not apparent until the mid-1950s, seven years after the messages "went public."

Immediately after the thirteenth apparition on October 4, 1947, Jeanne-Louise once more limped the two miles to the village priest at Plounevez-Lochrist to again tell what she had seen and heard. This time, though, the conversation between her and the priest "was overheard by a young girl who listened attentively" and then eagerly rushed to the village school with the details of the apparitions to Jeanne-Louise. From the school the news spread throughout the village, where "most didn't believe it." But some few nonetheless began "timidly going to pray in the meadow" near the house of Jeanne-Louise, and began asking her questions — and she began answering.

Jeanne-Louise began repeating all of the messages retained word for word in her memory. These included the stern admonishments given during the thirteenth apparition to the clergy for their failure to broadcast the messages, including the warnings and the calls to prayer.

Soon a small shrine was set up in the meadow. Flowers were deposited, and candles were lit. Small groups began attending, especially when Jeanne-Louise narrated the new messages, fourteen through twenty-one.

In late May 1949, a woman from Plounevez-Lochrist had become seriously ill. When she was brought to the hospital she was considered a desperate case with death imminent. Meanwhile, on May 24, some persons had decided to begin a novena at the small shrine which was by now called Our Lady of the Rosary of Kerizinen. During that novena the Holy Mother appeared to Jeanne-Louise for the twenty-second time. During this novena, some saw a "globe of light" descending over Jeanne-Louise's house.

After the apparition, Jeanne-Louise got the idea of using some of the flowers (apparently they were daisies) placed at the spot where the apparition had appeared in the meadow. After weaving the flowers into a wreath, she asked some of those present to carry them to the sick woman in the hospital at Plounevez-Lochrist.

These good people were denied entrance to the patient's room, but one of the attending sisters agreed to lay the flowers on the dying patient's bed. As soon as the flowers touched the bed, the dying woman began to speak, much to the astonishment of the attending sisters. Shortly her pulse and temperature were normal. She was cured.

As this news was broadcast, hardly anyone in the vicinity awaited for medical proof or a bishop's approval to call this a miracle. The site of the apparition was attended thereafter by increasing numbers of people.

On August 6, 1949, during the twenty-third apparition, Jeanne-Louise apparently pointed out to the Lady that the people of Kerizinen did not have any good drinking water and that it was necessary to walk nearly a mile to get some. The Lady promised that she would bring forth "a source to gush water." This did not happen for three years, but on July 15, 1952, some visitors passing through a bank of bushes to get to the meadow to pray stumbled upon some water coming down from the bushes.

When the brambles and ferns growing there were cut back, a vertical, artificially made "cave" was discovered, at the bottom of which there was a little water. As water was drawn out it was replaced by more water coming out of the rocks. The water was potable and is still flowing today, and many have claimed healing cures from it.

Apparitions twenty-four through twenty-eight followed. Then on December 8, 1953, about a thousand people were reciting the rosary under gray clouds and a thin rain. Even though Jeanne-Louise knelt and prayed, the Lady didn't appear. At three o'clock as the prayers and the Hail Marys came to an end, a "strange light attracted the eyes of all to the sky" — whereupon the clouds disappeared and a "very red sun detached itself from a part of the blue sky."

This sun, seeming to "fall down," witnessed by all those gathered, suddenly split into two parts. "The two halves began to turn in contrary directions one from the other, each one throwing out brilliant rays intensely colored and painting the same colors on everything in the neighborhood."

The same phenomena were witnessed by larger numbers again during May, August, and October of 1954 — except during the October display the "sun seemed to fall and emitted the same rays, but without splitting into two halves again." At one of these events what must have been exceedingly beautiful phenomena occurred:

It was as if a snow of light was flying around all of those in the meadow. The sky was serene, the air clean. The "snow-flakes" which looked like flower petals were formed at some height and were disappearing before touching the ground. The witnesses ran here and there to catch them, but their hands closed on air. Later this prodigy occurred again. At times there are perfumes that come by.

News of these remarkable phenomena, attested to by over a thousand witnesses, now began to radiate through Brittany and the rest of France.

Eventually Jeanne-Louise would experience at least seventy-one apparitions of the Lady. Some included secret messages not revealed, a few were similar to earlier occurrences, and sometimes the Holy Mother appeared but did not speak. During the twenty-fourth apparition, on December 9, 1949, however, the Lady told Jeanne-Louise:

> Go to your bishop. I want him to organize prayers and pilgrimages on this site, and that a chapel be built here. The miracles performed by my Son in former times here upon this very land, I want them to happen again, especially in favor of sinners.

Tradition had it that a monastery had long ago been built in the meadow of the apparitions and that Jesus had often appeared there.

Nonetheless, the bishop did nothing, and so some of the townspeople themselves constructed a small, forlorn shed-like structure on the site. Inside was placed a life-size statue of the Lady — which looked very little like the Holy Mother described by Jeanne-Louise. During the 1950s and 1960s crowds of five to six thousand would gather at this "chapel," especially on feast days, which must have been an embarrassment to the local clergy.

The request to the clergy for a chapel was occasionally repeated, to no avail. During the long thirty-first message of May 12, 1955, the Lady said, "Ask your bishop to establish in the parish an Association of the Children of Mary, which I have spoken of in earlier years." This referred to a sanctuary for poor children which presumably would have included a school and hospital.

This request was to cause much suffering to Jeanne-Louise, not only because the bishop would not officially receive it and turned his back on her when she dutifully attended communion, but because he increased his public declarations against the apparitions at Kerizinen.

It appears, then, that not only were the clergy at Kerizinen and Plounevez-Lochrist adamantly opposed to an apparition of the Holy Mother in their area, but also were inexplicably insensitive to the great economic benefits that a shrine might bring. There is no evidence that any official church inquiry ever took place regarding the astonishing events at Kerizinen.

The Holy Mother was effectively stalemated at Kerizinen — as ultimately acknowledged by the Lady herself. During the thirty-first apparition, on May 12, 1955, the Lady stated: "The devil has unchained all his malice so that my apparitions not be accepted in Brittany, but in spite of him I will triumph." This message impugns the local clergy and must have served to harden their resolve against the apparition.

In 1943, at the urging of her confessor, Jeanne-Marie began writing out the Lady's messages in her own hand, including the earlier ones, and gave the scripts to the priest. In the confusion that attended the revelation by the school girl in 1949, the scripts were somehow taken from the priest by some of the village people. Among these was found a description of the eleventh apparition on May 1, 1944.

On this date, Jeanne-Louise apparently had not seen the Lady herself, but was presented with an animated tableau. Part of the tableau showed men hoisting a red flag. Some priests were trying to stop them, but they were being threatened and abused, and stones were being thrown at them. In a corner was the devil, very happy, encouraging the men. In another corner was the Blessed Virgin crying. The tableau carried the inscription "The Image of Communism."

It must again be pointed up here that in 1944 the Soviet Communists were the much-appreciated allies of the West, while the general worldwide threat of Communism (also forewarned in 1917 at Fátima) was not fully realized until after 1953.

During 1961, Jeanne-Louise became increasing disabled and took to her house, where less frequent apparitions occurred. After 1978, obscurity descended over this holy apparition. Devout groups in Canada, France, and Belgium have worked to perpetuate the memory of holy events at Kerizinen, but apparently not at Kerizinen itself. A photo of Jeanne-Louise Ramonet published in 1978 shows her near the door of her humble house, dressed in peasant's cloths, supported by her cane and looking lonely.

13

Lipa, Philippines
(1948, 1949)

The Republic of the Philippines is composed of over seven thousand islands, only about four hundred of which are permanently inhabited. It is not far north of the Equator, and so the islands are hot and humid. The capital is Manila, situated on the eastern edge of a great and beautiful bay on the large island of Luzon. To the west of Manila Bay is the magical South China Sea.

In 1521, when Hernán Cortés was finally conquering the Aztec nobility in Mexico, the first of many Spanish expeditions reached the islands under the leadership of Ferdinand Magellan. The Filipinos were under Spanish rule for nearly four hundred years, and today about 84 percent of the population is Catholic.

During the early part of the twentieth century the rocky road to independence was followed with significant American support. Those efforts fluctuated until 1935, when the political powers involved agreed to establish a commonwealth. During that year General Douglas MacArthur became field marshal of the Commonwealth army. When World War II came suddenly to the islands in 1941, the Japanese occupied most of the islands and MacArthur was ordered out by President Roosevelt.

The people suffered enormously from Japanese brutality. The land and cities were devastated by war, the economy destroyed. The country was also torn by internal Filipino political wars and guerrilla violence. The retaking of the islands was extremely bloody, but on July 5, 1945, General MacArthur was finally able to announce that "all the Philippines are now liberated." Over five hundred thousand Japanese soldiers had died.

Now began the enormous problems of reconstruction amid local fighting for political and economic power. The Republic was declared in 1946, and arrangements for a plebiscite and military assistance from the United States were made in 1947.

In April of 1948, the first elected president of the republic died suddenly, elevating the vice-president, Elpidio Quirino, to the presidency. Quirino was bitterly resented. The turmoil was intense, and the people again suffered tremendously. It was amid this turmoil that a wondrous apparition of the Holy Mother occurred.

The town of Lipa (now called Lipa City) is found in the Batangas Province about sixty miles to the southeast of Manila. A little further along is the town of Rosario and then the seaside city of Batangas. Some forty-five thousand people in this area were killed during the Japanese occupation.

Lipa and Rosario are in the mountains about fifteen hundred feet above sea level. Lipa takes its name from the lipa tree, whose leaves and stems are "very itchy." Lipa and Rosario were once very important to the coffee trade. Coffee trees grew abundantly on the mountain slopes. But in 1889 an unforgiving type of smut destroyed all the trees. The coffee plantations didn't recover very well because of the political turmoil. So the inhabitants of Lipa were poor. The town had a Carmelite community whose nuns occupied an old monastery and did their best to minister to the needs of the poor. Among the nuns was the young Sister Teresita Castillo.

During the afternoon of September 12, 1948, Sister Teresita was alone in the enclosed courtyard garden. Sheltered in the interior courtyard there were some vines growing on the walls. She heard a voice calling her, and when she turned to see who it was she saw that a "small, white cloud" had formed in front of the vines. From the cloud emanated small rays of glittering light.

Apparently no image of the Lady was visible, and the voice spoke out of the cloud. "Fear not my child, kiss the ground. Whatever I shall tell you to do you must do. For fifteen consecutive days come to visit me here in this spot. Eat some grass." All of the subsequent messages rendered by the voice to Sister Teresita were short, and were shortest toward the end of the fifteen days.

The next day, a figure was seen in the cloud, one identifiable as the Lady. The following message occurred either on September 12 or September 13: "People believe not my words. Pray child, pray much because of persecution. What I ask here is exactly what I asked at Fátima. Tell this to the people."

It was immediately after the second appearance, on September 13, that a most remarkable phenomenon occurred. The day was clear but windy, the winds buffeting all the trees and shrubs in the vicinity. After the appearance, rose petals began falling from some point in the clear sky into the courtyard and elsewhere outside of the convent.

The rose petals floated down, drifting as if in their own vacuum, completely unperturbed by the winds. "Only after they came to rest did they obey the wind. Then, so profuse were they that they created large drifts as if it had snowed." Hundreds ran to gather them up, and their "fragrance was extraordinary."

Sister Teresita apparently completed the fifteen days of visits asked by the voice. At some point the Lady identified herself as "Mary, Mediatrix of All Graces" and asked that a shrine dedicated to her under this title be built upon the spot she had appeared. But the amazing phenomena had just begun.

The rose petals fell again during October. During November they fell for five consecutive days during heavy winds. They fell calmly until they touched the ground, and again an excited multitude ran here and there to gather them up.

A considerable amount of rose petals was accumulated this way and was dried and preserved. The rose petals were treasured, of course, once the news of the apparition had circulated. Many cures were reported when fragments of the petals were mixed with water and drunk.

The next year, during March 1949, many people from Lipa and Rosario claimed to have seen the face of the Holy Mother appearing on the surface of the sun. On March 23, there was a sudden commotion in the streets of Lipa. Looking upward, the entire town could see the Holy Mother standing among the clouds.

Around her figure were auras and auroras, colored lights appearing, glimmering, and disappearing — reds, blues, yellows, greens. The image was apparently three-dimensional, for some on one side of town reported seeing only the profile view, while those at the center saw the image face on. This gigantic apparition lasted for over two hours, time enough for more witnesses to arrive from Rosario, some of whom said they could see the image from two or three miles away.

A shrine was erected at the spot of the apparitions, as was also a chapel in Lipa City in honor of Our Lady, Mediatrix of All Graces. Rose petals, sealed in plastic, have been sent throughout the world.

14

Necedah, Wisconsin
(1949)

As we have seen, the apparitions of the Holy Mother tend to take place just prior to the emergence of war and deadly conflict. Now we come to the apparition at Necedah, Wisconsin, the first of the two American apparitions included in this book. Both were exceedingly complex affairs — among other reasons because they were ongoing for *years*. Moreover, Americans are not used to having apparitions of the Holy Mother take place in their country.

In 1949, the Cold War between the Soviet Union and the rest of the world was gaining momentum. Russia indeed was scattering "its [Communist] errors throughout the world," as first warned during the apparition at Fátima in 1917 and echoed by the apparition at Kerizinen in 1941. Harry S. Truman was president, and Joseph R. McCarthy had been elected senator from Wisconsin, later to become the infamous anti-Communist witch-hunter.

While praying on the winter night of November 12, 1949, Mary Ann Van Hoof, who was then forty, said she heard a "disturbance" in the hall. When she investigated she saw "something in the dark, sort of a white-like light." She first thought that it was one of her children, but then saw it was "a small figure with a veil on its head." She retreated into the bedroom. But the figure followed her. It stopped about four feet from the bed, where it watched her silently. "It was sort of bluish and light-colored in the front." Mary Ann was "terribly frightened."

Nothing more occurred until April 7, 1950, when she saw the CORPUS of the crucifix on the wall become "all aglow and twice its size," and a voice said, "Yes, pray my child. Pray, pray, pray hard. My child, your cross is heavy to bear, but the people all over the world are facing a heavier cross and sorrow with the enemy of God unless you pray. Pray hard with all your heart." The voice promised to return, not to the house, but outside "when the flowers bloom, and the trees and grass are green."

The biographical details of Mary Ann's early life caused many raised eyebrows when it came to considering her as an appropriate vehicle of the Holy Mother. The first forty years of the life of Mary Ann Van Hoof (nee Bieber) were unfortunate and hard. Born on July 31, 1909, she was the eldest of five children of Matthias Bieber and his wife, Elizabeth Gallman. Both were immigrants from eastern Europe and had married in Cincinnati in about 1907. Matthias, who was "mean" and anti-religious, suffered an injury to his hand while working for a steel company in Philadelphia. In 1914, Matthias settled his family on a small and unproductive farm in Kenosha County, Wisconsin.

As Mary Ann grew up, the herding and milking chores on the farm and in its "truck patch" prevented her from getting an education beyond the eighth grade. Later, she worked as a cook in a restaurant for long hours seven days a week. She attempted (and failed) to finance her own "resort hotel" from her own "meager wages." She married, but three months later, after she became pregnant, she discovered that the marriage was "a tissue of deception" since her new husband was already married. She was physically and mentally abused by this husband, and twice sustained serious physical harm requiring surgical operations.

"Her first valid marriage" came about after she answered an ad for a housekeeper and later, on July 3, 1934, married Fred Van Hoof, who had placed the ad. The Van Hoofs first had twins who didn't reach term, and then eight other children, one of whom died in infancy. The Van Hoof home was about three miles west of the village of Necedah. Near their home ran a railroad line which was to play a spectacular role during the continuing apparitions.

Whether the seer was religious before the apparition is not clear. According to Mary Ann, her father's violent antipathies to the church confused his children's understanding of religion. Her earlier religious interests were shallow. For two years she attended the Community Protestant Church of Pleasant Prairie, Kenosha County, Wisconsin, even though she had been baptized Catholic on "the sixteenth day after her birth on the feast of the Assumption in 1909."

She had wished to baptize her first child, born of the unfortunate bigamous marriage, but was "refused by the priest." Apparently while still working for Van Hoof as housekeeper, she undertook a three-week course in the Catholic religion — and was then "shriven, was married [to Van Hoof], made her First Communion, and had her baby baptized, all in the same day."

Many photographs exist of Mary Ann Van Hoof, both in ecstasy while kneeling before the apparition and under normal circumstances. Earlier ones depict a woman hardened by her life's difficult experiences; later photographs show her matronly and motherly, even serene.

Slightly different accounts exist regarding what happened on Pentecost Sunday, May 28, 1950. It seems that Mary Ann had just called her husband, who had been dozing in a chair, to dinner. One of her daughters, she said,

> . . . *was razzing me, kidding about something. I stooped over to brush a mosquito from my leg. I saw a flash of light, sort of like when the sun reflects across the windshield.*
>
> *Thinking a car drove up outside, I looked and saw a blue mist behind the four little ash trees out there, and something told me that this was the approach of a saint. At that time*

I always called her a saint because I didn't know who she really was.

I went out. And as soon as I went out, this blue mist floated through the tips of the trees and then formed into Our Lady. She lowered herself, smiling, with her arms extended.

The Lady positioned herself in the air about two feet off the ground — at a place afterward referred to as the "Sacred Spot" in the published literature.

The Lady was about five feet tall but her head was higher than Mary Ann's.

She had a blue veil on, blue robe, a cream-colored gown, with a golden cord around her neck which had on the one end the globe [of the earth] and on the other end a large tassel. And she had a large crucifix — large rosary in her hand with a crucifix about four or five inches.

The rosary beads were white, and on the crucifix "Our Lord is not nailed through the hands, He is nailed through the wrist. ...There is no braided crown of thorns around His head like we see in pictures."

Throughout the published materials are additional bits of information about what the Lady looked like. Her eyes were deep blue, her face was oval shaped, her chin rather pointed, her hair golden colored (at least what Mary Ann could see of it beneath the veil). "She stands on a cloud or pillow, with bare feet, with roses, pink roses around her feet." The Lady's arms seem always to be extended "as if she was going to embrace me as I walked toward her." Her blue robe had "some few gold stars near the bottom."

Mary Ann attested that she had never seen a picture or read a description that compared in any way with how the Lady was dressed. Furthermore she stated: "Oh, she was so radiant and beautiful, an artist couldn't paint her to do her justice." Nonetheless, artists soon tried to do so, some portraying the Lady without the blue robe and veil, and images of the apparition can be obtained at the shrine at Necedah.

When asked about how she heard the Holy Mother and what she was conscious of otherwise, Mary Ann answered: "Well, I'm pretty sure I heard it with the ears of my head. I don't know. I just hear. It seems she blots out everything. Like the family asked me a couple times if I noticed a train going by, which I didn't."

When asked if the messages might not be coming "from Our Blessed Lady" but from some diabolical source, Mary Ann replied:

Well, I've had those questions put to me before. Satan would not ask for the rosary. Satan would not give me the messages she does — that I have for the priests, and for the bishops and the pope. Those [messages] sure would not be the works of Satan, because he would just be doing the opposite instead of asking for prayer.

On May 29, 1950, the day after the Lady first appeared floating on the cloud, the Lady again came and spoke thus: "Wake up, America! The enemy of God is creeping all over America! *All* [emphasis added] religions must work together against the enemy of God! Pray! Pray! Pray for this. You must pray and convert Russia!"

In 1950 religions hardly worked together at all. Rather they had long traditions of fighting each other or at least surrounding themselves by thick ideological walls. Many religious leaders were aghast at this concept of interreligious cooperation. Nonetheless, the Holy Mother's messages at Necedah were taken down, mimeographed, and distributed to, among others, as many priests as possible.

Our Lady wondered why the people turned their backs on her and her messages given at other apparitions. And in her appearances on May 30, June 4, June 16, August 15, and October 7, the "Queen of Heaven" promised that she would return every year on those same days, and also on Trinity Sunday, for as long as Mary Ann lived.

The first major message at Necedah was delivered on June 16, 1950, at which time 1,425 people were gathered at the Van Hoof home and the Sacred Spot. This early gathering included a Father Lengowski, pastor of St. Francis Church, as well as Mass servers, and many photos were taken of the crowd. This message was something of a shock because, in no uncertain terms, it criticized the clergy:

> *To the priests of America, archbishops and bishops! There are too many of you whose desires in earthly goods and pleasures go before your duties. Humble yourselves, and be an example to your people. Remember you are workers of Christ here on earth. You must put more effort to call your flock back into the fold.*
>
> *For, if you will not hear me now, you, who are getting weak, will suffer terribly [from] violence and penance similar to the purged [Communist] countries. As you all know, the atomic bomb with its destruction is in the hands of the enemy [which was true but not publicly known at the time].*
>
> *Tell this to your priests and all other priests all over America and all over the world. There are too many priests who put luxuries and good times before their duties to God....*
>
> *Priests [Catholic] and ministers [Protestant?] must not war between themselves. Jealousies and hatred between religions is just what the enemy is looking for. Priests must be real shepherds, showing the way of Truth and the way of God's law regardless of religion and color.*

Copies of this message, printed by the organization that formed in service to this holy apparition, were boldly mailed to "all bishops at this time." And because of this distribution, the holy apparition at Necedah would never receive much in the way of official approval.

Some earnest debunking investigations were initiated by clergy, followed by imbroglios and flaps and stern priestly admonishments. Extensive official and unofficial probes got underway regarding Mary Van Hoof's "questionable" background and circumstances.

The fact that the Korean War began on June 25, 1950, nine days after the first major message at Necedah doesn't seem to have impressed Mary Ann's critics, most of whom tended to ignore the Lady's warnings about Communism. Yet by 1953 this particular scattering of "Russia's errors" was to take its toll on the United States with 54,000 dead and 103,000 wounded, while South and North Korean casualties were each at least ten times as high.

On the surface, it might have seemed that the whole affair was exceedingly questionable — "a transparent case of Mrs. Van Hoof's delicate state of mind." Commentary along that line was broadly published by priests and bishops in the news media in an effort to deflect public interest.

This debunking commentary, however, didn't achieve its purpose. During the apparition of June 16, the seer said that the Holy Mother had said that one hundred thousand people would attend the next promised apparition on August 15, 1950. This was to be two months after the June apparition, and the prediction was several times printed and distributed in advance. In fact, more than one hundred thousand arrived.

Indeed, so great had the demand grown for transportation to the Sacred Spot that the local railway company had begun scheduling special trains which would stop at the Van Hoof home to disgorge and retrieve passengers. The impressive August 15th Mass of pilgrims was photographed from airplanes as well as from the ground. The Wisconsin state police, now responsible for crowd control and management, "marvelled at the well-behaved crowd and not as much as a scratched fender."

On August 15, 1950, near noon, the seer knelt at the Sacred Spot surrounded by thousands of people, and the Holy Mother again appeared. At this point difficult problems emerge regarding how the messages of this and subsequent apparitions were recorded and put into print.

By 1982, eleven books and copious other materials and pamphlets had been published by the Queen of the Holy Rosary, Mediatrix of Peace Shrine at Necedah. Significantly missing in all of these sources is anything resembling a chronology of the continuing events.

To further complicate this matter, it appears that at each of the appearances the seer "saw and heard more than she had time to narrate while kneeling at the Sacred Spot." She then recalled bits and pieces of this additional material during subsequent questions and interviews. The chronology would be important regarding certain statements made by the seer and the authenticity of the Holy Mother's predictions.

For example, the literature indicates that immediately after the August 15, 1950, apparition, Mary Ann Van Hoof said that the Holy Mother had revealed to her that: "...the Enemy is in every branch of the government, the civil service, the news media, the armed service, the Pentagon, the priesthood, the Protestant ministry, bellhops in hotels...[The Virgin showed her] women spies who flew back and forth from city to city working for the enemy, their femininity gaining them access."

Mary Ann "also exposed the fact that thirty thousand Communists were trained as priests to infiltrate the Catholic Church. Ministers were also trained to infiltrate the Protestant churches and to strive for their destruction."

The 1950 date here is of some importance because it predates the forthcoming Communist scares that later were personified by Joseph McCarthy. In 1950, he was still an obscure Senator despite his anti-Communist blast against the State Department in February 1950. It was not until 1953–54 that he slowly gained visibility.

In this sense, the Lady's pronouncements through the seer about Communism were predictive — as also were the advance warnings of the forthcoming drug culture, the abortion issue, and "satanic" music and art, which did not get fully underway until about 1968.

All of these issues ultimately caused "rocks to be thrown at Mary Ann." But the biggest rocks of all were tossed because of the Lady's insistence that the religious denominations find ways of working together to combat the "Enemy," which was Communism. This request, or command, was reiterated during the August 15, 1950, apparition. Since the message is lengthy I will provide excerpts:

> *All religions must go together against the enemy of God, for he [the Enemy] is very strong right now. Remember your Commandments, the Way of the Cross — for the Enemy of God is all over America — you'd be surprised if the sheep's clothing were taken off and how they would spring up — all around you — even some that act like Christians — they have Satan in their hearts.*
>
> *... The priests cannot carry on alone — nor can the Catholics carry on alone. That's why all religions must work together, not in jealousy and hatred — but in love, Love thy neighbor — profanity and blasphemy hurts Our Lord.*
>
> *Bullets will only destroy and keep destroying.... But all of you must remember my warnings of Fátima, Lipa, and La Salette. I warned you then — I'm warning you again. ... [The] beginning [of the destruction?] is now in Korea; [but] it will not end there unless we pray. It's only beginning [in Korea] — half of America is involved with the Enemy of God.*

North Korea invaded South Korea in a surprise move on June 25, 1950. But it was generally thought that the North Koreans would respond to United Nations demands by withdrawing from South Korea. These hopes vanished when the North Koreans did nothing of the kind. So on June 30, 1950, President Truman authorized the use of American land, sea, and air forces in Korea in conjunction with an overall fifteen-nation United Nations effort.

The United Nations military counteroffensive war, headed by General Douglas MacArthur, began only on September 15, one month after the published prediction at Necedah. Indeed, the "beginning of the destruction" continued beyond the Korean conflict, and went on to involve Vietnam.

But this issue and others seemingly important to the Lady at Necedah were secondary to what the ecclesiastics saw as her most outrageous command: that the religions should work together. As Mary Ann Van Hoof often complained, it was this issue that caused most of the "rocks to be thrown" at her. It was clearly this issue that accounts for the lack of ecclesiastical support for or even mention of this great and intense American apparition.

On a Friday in Lent in 1951, in the presence of numerous people and cameras, Mary Ann Van Hoof received the stigmata of the Crown of Thorns, which was visible and photographed between 2:00 p.m. and 3:00 p.m. The same stigmata reoccurred on a Friday in Lent in 1952 under similar conditions, but didn't reoccur after that.

The holy wounds, examined by doctors, were "tangible surface and subcutaneous marks, and caused the seer considerable pain." These particular stigmata are indeed rare. They are understood to mean that the receiver is elected by the Most Holy to personify His Son's suffering — and, in this case, to confirm and dramatize the authenticity of the Lady who ultimately identified herself as Queen of the Holy Rosary, Mediatrix of Peace.

During the next Friday of Lent, in 1953, Mary Ann was placed in a hospital under the eyes of observing doctors, priests, and psychologists. Her hands were tied so that she could not somehow scratch the wounds into existence. The stigmata did not appear — and so the earlier ones were considered to have been somehow self-inflicted. But the Necedah devout held that this was like demanding that the Holy Mother produce the stigmata at the investigators' commands.

It is quite possible that without the stigmata the apparition at Necedah, and Mary Ann Van Hoof, might have passed into obscure apparitional history. Wisconsin ecclesiastical authorities ordered Mary Ann to be silent or suffer disciplinary action for disobedience.

However, pilgrims to the Sacred Spot could no longer be prohibited or even discouraged, whether the seer was silent or not. For the grassroots devout continued their enormous support for the Necedah apparitions, while the Sacred Spot and the Van Hoof home became a well-known tourist stop in Wisconsin.

Many analysts of the Necedah events imply that Mary Ann Van Hoof was unduly influenced by individuals around her. They also criticize her uneducated idioms and metaphors regarding forthcoming racial difficulties and Masonic conspiracies, her distinctions between the "true Jews" and "Yids," and so on.

When the United States entered the Vietnam war in 1961, this was seen by the Necedah devout as a further fulfillment of the August 15, 1950, prediction: "[Korea is] only the beginning — but it will not end there [until] half of America is involved with the Enemy of God!" Indeed, all America became involved with this expression of "Russia's errors" — costing fifty thousand American lives and over one million Vietnamese lives.

From the beginning miraculous cures, conversions, and witnessed miracles occurred at or near the Sacred Spot just outside the Van Hoof home. An extensive account of these between 1950 and 1966 was listed in *Testimonials of Pilgrims,* published by For My God And My Country, Inc.

The many cures do not seem to have impressed ecclesiastical authorities. But Mary Ann would submit to the ecclesiastical "silence" imposed on her. So in April 1974, Bishop Frederick Freking of La Crosse, Wisconsin, placed her, the Sacred Spot, the shrines which had been built, and six of her supporters under interdict. This is a Roman Catholic ecclesiastical censure withdrawing most sacraments and Christian burial from a person, location, or district. Mary Ann then went into hiding.

In 1975, though, the seer said that the Virgin Mary ordered her to break the interdiction and to continue her work and that the term "obedience" was "being used loosely by a church hierarchy that does not always follow the directives of the pope." This statement was heard over loudspeakers by about three thousand people who caught only a glimpse of Mary Ann standing in a doorway to bless the crowd.

Veneration of the apparition at Necedah has been a passionate grassroots effort. The shrines at Necedah consist of a complex of seven buildings donated by devoted workers' money and labor. Blueprints exist for larger structures. The Shrine of the Queen of the Holy Rosary, Mediatrix of Peace, produces extensive amounts of literature.

Mary Ann Van Hoof died in 1984.

15

Jerusalem, Israel
(1954)

Jerusalem, now the capital of modern Israel, is a most ancient site of the former Palestine area. Some scholars believe it to have been the city of Salem mentioned in the Book of Genesis. It was called Urusalim in the Tel El Amarna tablets of about 1400 B.C.E. It was also called Jebus, probably from the name of its early inhabitants. In 1048 B.C.E., David captured the Jebusite fortress of Zion, made it his capital, and brought there the Ark. Under the glorious period of Solomon, that king built the great Temple on the Mount and surrounded the city with vast walls.

Thereafter followed a succession of invasions by the Egyptians, the Arabians, and the Babylonians — each of whom sacked the city and carried the inhabitants into captivity and slavery. The city lay in waste until under Cyrus the Jews were allowed to return and the city was rebuilt. It was again razed in 168 B.C.E. by Antiochus Epiphanes, and the people were slaughtered. The Hasmoneans then revolted, rose in power, and established the Maccabean dynasty, which remained in power until the rule of Herod.

During Herod's reign there occurred the events in the life of Jesus which were to make Jerusalem the Holy City of the Christian world. Herod made Jerusalem into a Roman city, beautifying it with new buildings, including a rebuilt version of the temple. The city was completely destroyed after being taken by Titus in

70 C.E. Emperor Hadrian built a new city in 130 C.E., from which the Jews were banned.

During the time of the Emperor Constantine the city became a Christian shrine under its old name, Jerusalem. Constantine's mother, Helena, had churches built on the traditional sacred sites, including the Church of the Holy Sepulchre in the temple area on what was believed to be the tomb of Jesus. In 615, the city was besieged and sacked by the Persians, and in 637 it passed to Omar, who built in the same temple area the beautiful Moslem mosque called the Dome of the Rock, quite near the Holy Sepulchre.

In 1099, after terrible slaughters, the Crusaders defeated the Moslems and made Jerusalem the capital of the Latin Kingdom. However, it was recovered by Saladin in 1187 and remained in Moslem possession until the British took active control of Palestine in 1927. The principal problems at that time were the relations between the Arabs and the Jewish immigrants supported by extensive foreign capital. The bitter antagonisms extended into every facet of life, and the British were forced to govern by arbitrary rule.

This terrible situation obtained until November 1947, when the United Nations recommended a "Plan" which would turn Palestine into a Jewish state and an Arab state, with a small internationally administered zone which included Jerusalem. The Plan was accepted by the Israelis and most of the rest of the world, but not by the Arabs. Nonetheless, the British high commissioner soon departed, and the State of Israel was proclaimed at Tel Aviv in May 1948. Wars and atrocities occurred which soon involved the entire Middle East and which are more or less ongoing today behind the "Peace Process."

Jerusalem is sacred to Jews, Christians, and Moslems; the center of Christian veneration is the Holy Sepulchre. Officially called the Church of the Resurrection, it is situated, according to tradition, on the site of Jesus' tomb and is connected with chapels of St. Helena and the Inventions of the Cross, where the True Cross is said to have been found.

The church itself was refurbished by the Crusaders, and in 1810 it was generally improved and rearranged by the Eastern Orthodox, who control the larger part of its collection of buildings. There are many chapels and partitioned sections for the use of Roman Catholics, Copts, Syrian Jacobites, and Gregorian Armenians. Under this complicated arrangement, the possession of the Holy Sepulchre has always been a matter of bitter contest.

The Coptic Patriarchal Church and the Coptic School of St. Anthony of Egypt are barely a hundred yards from the Holy Sepulchre. In these surroundings there occurred two apparitions of the Holy Mother during two weeks in July 1954. These appearances are important to the history of the Holy Mother's apparitions because they had very many witnesses.

On the morning of July 18, 1954, Primary Class Five was receiving religious instruction at the School of St. Anthony. The young students included Coptic, Catholic, and Moslem children. At about 11:00 a.m. as the students were anticipating lunch break, some of them were looking out the window. Suddenly, they exclaimed with excitement: "El Adra! El Adra!" (The Virgin!)

She was there, they shouted, across the courtyard floating by a window. The Lady was recognized as the Virgin because she was dressed in blue and was surrounded by an aura which was glowing white near her body, but turned iridescent blue as it radiated outward.

All of the children rushed to the windows to see the sight, and all saw the Lady. The teacher, however, did not, but couldn't get the children to come away from the windows and settle down. So the school secretary was summoned. The secretary apparently could not see the Lady across the courtyard, so he commanded the children to stop being silly, and after bringing the class back to order he locked the door to prevent them from going into the courtyard.

Soon the children were in an uproar again. This time the Lady appeared in the classroom among them. Some say she floated, and others that she walked on the floor. She and her whitish-blue aura seem to have been transparent since the young witnesses could see right through her.

This event lasted for about five minutes, or at least long enough to attract several adults. These could not see her at first. But then the Lady stationed herself in front of one of the classroom walls, where she grew in intensity and brilliance. At that point, several of the adults said they could see a faint luminescence and an outline of a figure. Then the Lady disappeared. The news was quickly spread about. The school was permanently disrupted for that day, and hundreds came to view the classroom.

The Coptic Patriarchal church connected with the School of St. Anthony experienced a sudden increase of visitors and pilgrims. Scheduled services were standing-room only. Thus, one week later there, on July 25, were between two hundred and four hundred people present in the church at Vespers, including Moslems as well as Christians.

As the priest, "a tough, strong, no-nonsense man," was conducting the service, almost the entire congregation started shouting and crying out. When the priest looked up he "was so overcome that he could not continue the service." For he, as well as everyone else attending, clearly saw the apparition of the Holy Mother moving either just above the heads of everyone, or among and between them.

This time the Lady was less transparent then before, and some rays of colored light streamed out from her and bathed the astonished faces with colors, which also reflected on the walls. This appearance lasted for about fifteen minutes, which was enough time to call in others — most of whom also saw her. Then she slowly faded until only her blue-white aura was present, and then that too faded and disappeared.

An account of these two apparitions appeared in the *Coptic Patriarchal Journal*. But the Copts "showed no inordinate pride," nor did they "think themselves favored." "She did not come for our sakes," said the bishop. "She came because this place is holy, being within a few yards of Calvary and the Tomb."

The classroom where the first appearance took place was painted in blue, which was said to match the Lady's dress, and a magnificent icon of the Holy Mother was placed on the wall in front of which she had appeared. A plaque outside the window records the events.

After this apparition, the ongoing Israeli and Arab troubles reached new heights, especially in the Gaza area in 1955 and 1956, despite United Nations intervention.

On October 29, 1956, provoked by fierce Arab threats of invasion, Israel made a preemptive attack on Egyptian territory. Within a few days, Israel conquered the Gaza Strip and the Sinai peninsula. Britain and France invaded the area of the Suez Canal to keep it from being destroyed. United Nations troops were eventually sent to keep peace between Egypt and Israel.

16

Garabandal, Spain
(1961)

In 1961 Spain was still suffering the enormous political and economic repercussions of its Civil War (1936–39), a war fomented by Spanish Loyalists and Fascists against Socialists and Communists who had risen to power. The Fascists vanquished the Communists and under the leadership of Francisco Franco set up a dictatorship. The church was restored to its favored position and regained its property, although there continued to be much friction between church and state.

In the early 1960s, the church, tactfully silent for a long time, began to voice objections to aspects of the dictatorship. The last thing the church authorities wanted was a much publicized apparition of the Holy Mother.

Garabandal was yet another of those out-of-the-way places the Lady seems to favor. It lies some 250 miles west of Lourdes, France, in the Cantabrian Mountains at an elevation of about two thousand feet. The nearest large city is Santander on the Bay of Biscay. Garabandal is a cluster of buildings sitting rather humbly atop a high hill, itself in a kind of valley clinging to the sides of other hills. The landscape is dry and rocky, with a few trees. The town's few buildings, closely nestled together, are made of rock with tile roofs.

On June 18, 1961, after church in the evening, four young girls had just stolen some apples from a tree and had fled into a rocky ravine, a *calleja,* to eat them and contemplate "making the devil happy and our guardian angels sad."

The *calleja* was a rock-lined depression five or six feet deep, which became a waterway when it rained. Its path ran from the village up a low hill topped by a few pine trees. Many of the future apparitions would take place in the *calleja,* or near The Pines, and others in the parish church. The young girls were Conchita González, Loli Mazón, and Jacinta González, each twelve years of age, and María Cruz González, age eleven. The González girls were not related.

Suddenly, a very beautiful figure appeared, shining brightly without hurting their eyes. The girls fled back to town, frightened. They told about what they had seen, and the usual responses occurred: the girls were scolded for getting home late, and the parents were angry with them and their "silly story."

What they had seen, they said, was an angel, with very strong build, yet with a very young face like a boy of nine or so. He looked very masculine, with a brilliance about him too beautiful to explain, and a large, almost transparent pink-reddish set of wings. Or rather they were not exactly wings, not exactly attached to his body, but like a halo gleaming from behind him. He wore a long blue tunic. He had dark eyes and tan skin. He was very beautiful.

Family and friends began explaining him away — a large bird, maybe a little boy, maybe they were dreaming. The next day, the parish priest, Father Valentín Marichalar, came to discuss the event. After the priest found he couldn't convince the girls that they were mistaken, he suggested that if they saw the Angel of Peace (so dubbed by the girls) that night, they should ask who he was and why he was coming.

The four girls returned to the *calleja,* followed by some boys who were teasing them, some even throwing stones. Other people followed along too. But nothing happened. Later when Conchita was home in bed saying her prayers, she heard: "Don't be troubled. You will see me again." The other girls had heard the same message. So they went to the *calleja* again — and then again.

The angel reappeared to them eight times in all. At some point, all four girls began going into ecstasy, and their heads would simultaneously snap upward. They were pricked with pins, but they felt no pain. The last appearance of the angel was on July 1, 1961. By now the town had set up safety barriers to keep the crowds from falling down the rocks and the sides of the *calleja*. As the girls knelt, many others knelt also and began praying with them. The angel reappeared, and was smiling.

"I have come to announce to you a visit by the Virgin," he said, "under the title of 'Our Lady of Mount Carmel,' who will appear to you tomorrow, Sunday."

This electrifying news was communicated quickly, so the next day was a very busy one in the small hamlet. Cars were parked everywhere possible, and the overflow extended to nearby open areas. A large number of people were ambling about. Some were in tears and had brought gifts to the four surprised seers. By six in the evening, the crowd of people, including a dozen priests and several doctors, followed the girls to the *calleja*. The "mood of the crowd was thick, silent, and expectant."

"Our Blessed Mother" appeared to the girls as promised. As they described, the Blessed Mother was "like no other woman." She wore a long white dress covering her feet, with a blue mantle and a crown of golden stars. Her skin color was lighter than the two angels who accompanied her, but yet dark — different. Her hair was dark chestnut brown and wavy. The face was oval-shaped with fine features, beautiful lips, and a delicate Roman nose. Her voice "was too lovely to describe." Her hands were open and moving. She wore the brown scapular of Our Lady of Mount Carmel. She appeared as three-dimensional, physically solid, and with an intimate, natural presence — as the girls said, "just like you and me."

The Lady was accompanied by two angels on each side of her who were not like "you and me." They "looked like twins," were dressed exactly alike in long, seamless blue robes, and had big pink wings. "The faces were neither long nor small." Their eye color was black and penetrating, and they had fine hands and short fingernails. They looked about nine years old, but nevertheless "they gave the impression of being very strong." One was St. Michael, the other St. Gabriel.

Next to the angel who stood to the right of the Virgin, the children saw "an eye of great size." The eye appeared framed in a triangle, itself framed in a red square. There was also some writing in "an odd Oriental script." Some have dubbed this eye as the "Eye of God."

A lengthy conversation now took place, in which the girls told the Blessed Mother about the details of their daily lives. But something now happened which was generally considered "uncanny." The four girls seemed physically to change and become beautiful and serene, as if some kind of deep inner beauty had come alive within them. Their eyes were bigger and limpid and calm, free of any hints of the universal pain of the poor and disenfranchised. This dramatic change was immediately noticed by almost everyone. Indeed, in the thousands of photos later taken of the girls either in their ordinary state or in ecstasy, this subtle beauty is striking and quite apparent.

The appearances of the Blessed Mother were to occur for the next five years. Some sources indicate that the appearances numbered as high as two thousand. The events occurred almost daily.

Because of the number of appearances, a very large devotional literature has accumulated. But unlike most of the other great speaking apparitions, at Garabandal the Lady seldom addressed world affairs. There were no references that concerned the seers personally and no secrets of wider scope that were to be revealed at some future time.

Laced through the many messages, however, were intimations of three future events, which became known as a "great miracle," a "warning," and a "chastisement." The latter two events have apocalyptic overtones, but the events were not described beyond those three words. As will be seen below, these three events were to be given fuller description during the apparitions which took place at Bayside, New York, beginning in 1970.

Many of the messages were personal ones for pilgrims who came to Garabandal, a unique phenomenon in the history of apparitions.

There were three main witnessed phenomena which marked the history of this small village between the summer of 1961 and June 1965. The first of these phenomena has to do with "the Calls." Although the children did not at first speak of it, many soon noticed that when the girls were expected to go to the *calleja* or The Pines they did not go. When they were questioned about this, they said "We haven't been called yet."

At other times, the four girls, although in separate parts of the village, would simultaneously respond to the call, joining each other along the way. Wherever they were, separately or together, all heard the call by some "interior voice." Apparently each went into some kind of mild ecstasy on hearing the call. So when villagers and pilgrims noticed any of them hurrying along in this manner they knew that the Blessed Mother had summoned them again.

The second phenomenon has to do with "medical statements," of which many accumulated before "the doctors gave up." These four young seers were many times poked, prodded, and "tested" during their ecstasies. The more profound ecstasy-trance could come on quite suddenly, so that the girls would violently fall to their knees and people worried that they had broken bones or cut their knees on the rocks.

Coming out of the trance was just as sudden, and the girls simply came to an upright position at the exact same time — as would also be the case with the seers at Medjugorje, Yugoslavia, beginning in 1981.

Between 1961 and 1962, a large number of medical doctors submitted the entranced girls to "most painful cuts, brutal shaking, and even burns" — none of which ever served to bring them out of their ecstasies and "back to their normal senses." Flash-lights were put directly to their eyes, but not a flicker of an eyelid or pupil was to be seen.

Chief among those investigators was a Dr. Ortiz of Santander, a children's specialist, who spent twenty-two consecutive days studying the girls. He was convinced that a normal or abnormal psychological explanation was unthinkable. A Dr. Puncernau, who became one of the top medical authorities on Garabandal, saw the girls in ecstasy some twenty times and examined them very thoroughly both in and out of ecstasy. He concurred that there was "neither a normal nor a pathological explanation for the happenings."

The third phenomenon was sometimes called the "Prodigy of the Host" or the "Miracle of the Forma." During their ecstasies, the four young girls were the most photographed, tape-recorded, and filmed seers of all time up to then. On many occasions, the girls stuck out their tongues, later explaining that they were being given communion by an angel and that the host was placed on their tongues. The host was always invisible though.

On July 3, 1962, the Virgin told Conchita, "The miracle will occur on July 18th — as you say the *milagruco,* or little miracle." Of course, the massive numbers of pilgrims and observers had demanded a miracle, and all were expecting something along the lines of those at Fátima.

On July 18, the word of the forthcoming miracle having spread throughout Spain, the village of Garabandal found itself packed with pilgrims and cars and busses. The "little miracle" took place late at night, outside, under the glow of the moon and manifold flashlights and was recorded on film.

Walking to the designated site, The Pines, Conchita suddenly fell to her knees and stuck out her tongue as if to take commu-nion. On her tongue there materialized a glowing host, which remained visible for two minutes in keeping with the angel's re-quest that it should be visible to everyone until the Virgin made her appearance.

And indeed, the host was visible to everyone near enough to see it and was captured on film as a small orb of glowing white light.

The film has withstood all attempts to debunk it or reveal some logical explanation for the appearance on celluloid of the host.

Many miraculous cures also took place, and during the course of the numerous events, most of which were at night, many spectators claimed they witnessed celestial phenomena. These, however, do not seem to have been as pronounced as those which occurred at other apparitions.

Even so, the apparitions at Garabandal were popularly accepted as authentic. The responses of various religious authorities, however, were another matter. From the start of the events at Garabandal, the bishops at Santander had refused to admit the divine origin of the events. The sheer number of accumulating events and messages ensured that the "investigation would be a long one."

To further complicate this matter, though, the Holy Mother castigated segments of the church during what became known as the "Second Formal Message" on June 18, 1965. On that day, the seers were accompanied by about two thousand people, many from France, Germany, England, Italy, the United States, and Poland.

The message, given via the Archangel Michael and immediately heard by the crowd, read in part: "Many priests are on the road to perdition and are taking many souls with them. The Holy Eucharist is being given less importance [honor]. We must avoid God's anger with us by our efforts at amendment."

The commission set up by the bishop at Santander said, via a press release issued on July 8, 1965, that "although there was nothing to be condemned in the teachings, the messages and counsels of Garabandal, the commission did not think there was conclusive and definite proof of the supernatural character of all that had happened there." Further, to avoid giving the impression that the church had already approved anything, priests were "forbidden to go there without permission."

Conchita was called to Rome by Cardinal Ottaviani and went there in January 1966 accompanied by her mother and a priest. She visited the Holy Office and spent two and a half hours there in "a very cordial interview." A few days later, she was received privately by Pope Paul VI, who, during his conversation with her, said: "I bless you, and with me the whole church blesses you."

This was not taken as approval of Garabandal, but the blessing was not without significance. Shortly thereafter, a special emissary from the Holy Office was sent to Garabandal to investigate the apparitions and question the witnesses of the phenomena. The investigations went on for some time, but apparently no official report was made available.

During the early apparitions, the girls had already been pressed to request of the Lady a "great miracle" which would act as public proof of the divine origin of their experiences so "that people would believe them." As the girls told the Lady, "At Lourdes and Fátima you gave them proof." The Lady "looked grave" each time the request was put to her.

During the apparition on the night of June 19, 1961, four weeks after the first appearance of the Holy Mother, a Jesuit Friar, Luis María Andreu, was present at The Pines, and apparently didn't believe in what was happening. When he looked upward he experienced seeing a "Miracle!" and uttered the word four times.

Friar Luis was thirty-six and healthy, but he inexplicably died in the car while returning from Garabandal. It was said that he died "of excessive joy resulting from the sharing in the vision and the preview of the great miracle."

During 1963 and 1964, Conchita indicated that the "great miracle" would occur and would be seen by Padre Pio at San Giovanni Rotondo in Italy and by the pope at Rome. She also said that after the miracle the body of Friar Luis Andreu would be found incorrupt.

The "great miracle" had not occurred when Padre Pio died in September 1968. In 1978, the Jesuit seminary where Friar Luis had been a professor of theology and where he was buried was converted into an asylum. This necessitated the removal of all the graves — and it was discovered that the body of Friar Luis had been reduced to a skeleton.

The last apparition at Garabandal took place on November 13, 1965, to Conchita, who was called to The Pines and went there alone during a heavy rain. The Holy Mother, warning of difficulties to come unless all tried to do better, indicated she would appear no more — and this long and complicated cycle of apparitions at Garabandal was closed.

The four young seers grew up and led normal lives, but refused to benefit economically in any way from their reputations. The events at Garabandal became well known throughout Europe, England and Ireland, and the United States.

17

San Damiano, Italy
(1964)

The political shifts of Italy have always been complicated. As of 1963, the Italian political scene was divided between the Christian Democrats and the Socialist Democrats, intertwined with Communist, Vatican, and alleged Mafioso influences, which inspired "considerable uncertainty." The intrigues of this mixture were temporarily resolved when Aldo Moro of the center-right became prime minister in 1963. The Moro government was wobbly, as most Italian governments were.

An apparition of the Holy Mother occurred in 1964. It was impressive for several astonishing phenomena, among which were the first photographs of one of the Holy Mother's apparitions.

There are two other San Damianos in Italy, but this third one is yet another out-of-the-way place not found in standard atlases. The third one, referred to as a village, is found in a mountainous area about forty-five miles to the southeast of Milan.

In the village lived Rosa Quattrini, wife of Giuseppe, and locally known as "Mamma Rosa." During 1961 she had been suffering from advanced intestinal tumors, having several times been hospitalized at Piacenza. During the last hospitalization her tumors had perforated the intestinal walls and she quickly developed incurable peritonitis, a deadly and painful disease. Mamma Rosa was sent home to die. She was fifty-two.

On September 29, 1961, while tended by her Aunt Adele, she lay abed in excruciating pain. A "lady visitor" came to the house asking for donations for Padre Pio, the famous friar of the Capuchin monastery at San Giovanni Rontondo, near Foggia.

Padre Pio was known to possess notable powers of clairvoyance and precognition and had demonstrated stigmata wounds. However, he tried his best to avoid public notice and humbly devoted himself to good works for the poor. Even so, his phenomena and works were not accepted by the Holy Office, but were widely accepted by the public.

The visitor was described as a young woman about twenty-five years old, very beautiful, more blonde than brunette. She was dressed in a poor bluish-gray dress and carried a black purse. She said she came from far away.

The woman asked Aunt Adele's permission to visit Rosa. When the church bell at San Damiano rang out the Angelus, the lady asked Rosa to say it with her. After that, the lady asked Rosa to get out of bed and offered her hand to help Rosa to stand up. The visitor then placed her hand on the afflicted parts of Rosa's body. At this, Mamma Rosa's pains immediately ceased — and she was cured both of the peritonitis and the perforating tumors. This miraculous cure was later medically confirmed, to the astonishment of everyone.

As Rosa knelt in tears before the lady, the latter told her to go to San Giovanni Rontondo and present herself to Padre Pio, which Rosa soon did after fully recovering and raising the money to get to San Giovanni Rontondo.

After Rosa arrived there, the same young woman appeared to her and told her that she was the Mother of Consolation and the Mother of the Afflicted. She herself conducted Rosa to Padre Pio and then disappeared. On the instructions of Padre Pio, Rosa consecrated herself to the care of the sick in the hospital at Piacenza.

❈

About two years later, Padre Pio interrupted Rosa's work of caring for the sick and revealed to her that she must return to her home, where a very important mission awaited her. Rosa arrived back at San Damiano at some point in 1963, but nothing of the "important mission" was apparent until October 16, 1964.

On that day, while Mamma Rosa was again saying the Angelus, she heard herself called by a voice outside the house. Going outside, she encountered "an apparition of the Blessed Virgin" suspended in the air over a pear tree. The Virgin told her she would come to see her every Friday and would give messages "to transmit to the world."

To prove the truth of her appearance, the Lady said that she would "give signs," the first of which would be making the pear tree bloom out of season. She asked that a well be dug right next to the tree — and then disappeared.

Even though Rosa's cure and her sponsorship by Padre Pio had given her special distinction, still everyone was dubious — for pear trees blossomed only in the spring, and it was October. Yet, as dawn came the next day, all found the pear tree loaded with flowers which produced a very strong and sweet fragrance.

This phenomenon created a sensation. For seventeen days thousands of curious spectators and the press were able to admire the phenomenon, and hundreds of photos were taken and published in the media. (The same tree again bloomed in late September of the next year.)

The well was quickly dug — and produced "miraculous water." From this water, people were soon being cured of blindness, deafness, paralysis, and other ailments, while many others were "cured of diseases of the soul."

On the following Friday, watched by a considerable number of people, over the pear tree the Lady again appeared to Rosa — as she was to do on every Friday *for the next thirteen years.*

Mamma Rosa was born in January 1909 at Sentimento de Rottofreno to Federico and Giacomina Buzzini. Of the seven children born, only four daughters survived childhood. The life of Rosa and her sisters consisted of school and farm work. Federico (and the Buzzini clan) was very devout and pious. He died when Rosa was two.

Rosa was to marry, but her three sisters each joined religious orders. One ended up in Brazil as a missionary, another one in Ceylon working among lepers, and the third became a Carmelite nun. The three sisters were happy and grateful that Rosa was favored as a vehicle of the Holy Mother.

Photos of Mamma Rosa show a plump woman, humbly dressed in the somber, traditional "uniform" of Italian peasant women.

It seems that during the apparitions over the famous pear tree the Lady was seen by Rosa dressed in various ways, including red — a color inconsistent with standard versions of the Blessed Virgin Mary. But the Lady either stood on roses or they floated around her; hence she became known as "Our Lady of the Roses." During the apparition of November 9, 1969, the Lady said:

> *I will come dressed in red three times, as today. After these three times the Eternal Father will act in justice, if you [erring humanity?] do not ask pardon, if you do not make amends for all these sins and sacrileges.*

At this, Mamma Rosa, in her "slight trance," thus reported:

> *The Mother has arrived at the pear tree, clothed all in red, in a light so great and resplendent that it shines upon the whole world — with all the angels accompanying her and also the martyred saints who have given their lives for Jesus.*

The Holy Mother delayed other "signs" until the appearance on December 8, 1967, the feast of the Immaculate Conception. On that day about two thousand persons were present. At least half were from foreign countries — France, Switzerland, Germany, Yugoslavia, Austria, the United States, Canada, and several South American countries.

The crowd observed a sun "spinning for half an hour and throwing out multi-colored rays. It was completely darkened and only the outer ridge could be visible...like an eclipse." (There were no eclipses during December 1967.) Many photographs were taken of these phenomena.

On December 9, 1968, the *Piacenza Daily Newspaper* was able to report on its front page: "One hundred and fifty busses and about a thousand cars brought a tremendous crowd of people to San Damiano yesterday. According to the best estimates there were about ten thousand people.... About thirty French priests were there around the pear tree."

Rain had fallen during the night before and was still falling on the crowd. All approaches to San Damiano were clogged with parked cars and busses. And so thousands of people with umbrellas had to trudge through ankle-deep mud to get to the pear tree — or as close to it as they could. The crowd around Mamma Rosa and the tree was very dense.

At a certain point, Mamma Rosa requested that everyone close their umbrellas. Then, as at Fátima in 1917, several signs commenced, which were variously to take place during a number of apparitions. To name but a few, they are described as: twirling suns; the doubling of the sun; white illuminated crosses in different positions, some with the spinning sun at the intersection of the vertical and horizontal bars of the cross; perfect circles made up of little rays resembling icicles; a perfect circle of ten beads; rays in different shapes and forms; rectangles and triangles in the sky or behind the sun; bars or columns in vertical or horizontal positions across entire photographs; hexagons; an image of a monk suspended in the air.

Scores of photos were taken of these phenomena, both in black and white and in color. A number of these were "very seriously and diligently examined" by Dr. Pierre Weber, research engineer at the National Office for Study and Research in Air and Space at Paris. Specialists in different fields of meteorology and film analysis examined other photos.

None could discover a natural cause for the phenomena photographed. Since no natural explanation could be found, they and subsequent specialists lapsed into silence and gave up the quest to discover a natural explanation. None of the specialists, however, would venture conclusions that incorporated a supernatural explanation, so skeptics were free to say the photos were either fake or reflected natural atmospheric phenomena of mysterious origin.

Many people had been photographing the area over the top of the pear tree where Mamma Rosa said the Holy Mother appeared. At the appearance on October 17, 1967, some of the resulting photos revealed the ultimate "sign" — a luminous, but slightly foggy shape. It was clearly recognizable as a woman dressed in a long gown and outlined by a brilliant aura. The bottom part of the photos usually show the top leaves and branches of the pear tree.

The devout were very impressed, but skeptics denounced the photos as fakes. The San Damiano photos never really recovered from this condemnation, even later, in 1968, when the famous photographs at Zeitoun, Egypt, were taken. Since the luminous apparitions there were directly observed by at least five hundred thousand people, the Zeitoun photos were never contested. The San Damiano photos of the image are nearly identical to those taken at Zeitoun.

Throughout the course of the many messages at San Damiano, the Holy Mother again expressed unhappiness with erring humankind. These messages generally follow the theme of "the devil is rampant everywhere in the world." For example, on March 25, 1970: "I am insulted in this place [i.e., the world], I am so scorned, blasphemed! This causes me much sorrow because humanity does not see that I come to save all."

Some of the messages refer to a universal apocalypse to come unless the world changes its sinful ways. During the message of September 9, 1969, the Holy Mother said: "And do not fear, my dear children, because I will come, yes, I will come into your midst and everyone will see me — and will then believe." This is taken to refer to great appearances yet to come — although in 1969 the apparition at Zeitoun, Egypt, had already been underway for a year.

On December 29, 1966, while the apparitions of the Holy Mother to Rosa Quattrini were in progress, the Sacred Congregation for the Doctrine of the Faith in Rome decreed that ecclesiastical permission was no longer required for publication about revelations, visions, or miracles, or for frequenting nonrecognized places of apparitions. The decree, approved by Pope Paul VI, also stated:

> *There is hence no longer any prohibition concerning the narrative of seers, be they recognized or not, by ecclesiastical authority.... It is permitted for Catholics to frequent places of apparitions, even those not recognized by the ordinaries of the dioceses or by the Holy Father.*

During her May 7, 1970, message, the Holy Mother promised: "I am always here with you, night and day. As long as my instrument is alive, I will always be here." And so it was, every Friday until Mamma Rosa Quattrini, the "instrument" of Our Lady of the Roses at San Damiano, died on September 5, 1981. She was buried in "the odor of sanctity" on September 8, 1981, the traditional birthday of the Blessed Virgin Mary.

18

Montichiari, Italy
(1947, 1966)

Montichiari ("Bright Mountains") is found on the fertile plain of the River Po, about sixty miles to the northeast of San Damiano, with the beautiful Lake Guarda about six miles farther on against the backdrop of the Italian Alps. The nearest large city is Brescia, about fourteen miles to the northwest of Montichiari.

Attached to Montichiari is a suburb called Fontanelle, and it was there that Pierina Gilli was born on August 3, 1911. Her biographical data are sketchy, but during the spring of 1947 when she was thirty-five, she was working in a hospital in Montichiari proper. World War II had ended not long before, and Italy was rebuilding.

Pierina was working alone in a room at the hospital when a beautiful woman suddenly appeared before her. She "wore a violet dress and a white veil around her head. She was very sad, and her eyes were filled with tears which fell to the floor. Her breast was pierced by three big swords."

The Lady said only three words: "Prayer — Penitence — Expiation." Thereafter she was silent, but her tears fell in glittering drops. She then vanished.

On June 13, 1947, a Sunday, the Lady returned early in the morning. This time she was dressed in white and instead of the three swords had three roses — white, red, and golden-yellow. Pierina asked: "Please tell me who you are."

The Lady smiled: "I am the Mother of Jesus and the Mother of all of you." The Lady then gave some rather lengthy instructions regarding new devotions toward her and new arrangements for religious orders and priests. She wished the thirteenth of each month to be celebrated as the Day of Mary, and on this day she would give to those who honored her "a superabundance of graces and great sanctity." She wished the thirteenth of each month to be celebrated in honor of the "Rosa Mystica," the mystical rose.

She now explained the meaning of the three swords which had pierced her breast during the first appearance: the first sword: loss of the vocation of a priest or monk; the second sword: priests, monks, and nuns who lived in deadly sin; the third sword: priests and monks who commit the treason of Judas, who, while giving up their vocation, also lose their faith and their eternal beatitude and become enemies of the church.

The Lady then explained the meanings of the three roses: the white one meant the spirit of prayer; the red one, the spirit of expiation and sacrifice; the golden one, the spirit of penitence.

The third appearance occurred on October 22, 1947; during it the Lady stated: "My divine Son, tired of the continuing offenses, wanted to act according to His justice. So I placed myself as a mediatrix between Him and the human race, especially for the consecrated souls."

The fourth appearance was in the parish church on November 16. Some other people were present and either saw the apparition or saw Pierina fall into a mild ecstasy. "Our Lord, my divine Son, is tired of the many offenses, the severe offenses, the sins against holy purity," the Lady said. Then, after a pause, she continued: "He wants to send another flood or punishment. I have interceded. I ardently ask the priests to admonish the people in love that they do not commit these sins any more." Three more appearances were to follow.

Meanwhile, people had heard of the appearances. One family brought to the church a boy of about five who was suffering from polio and could not stand or walk. Another family brought their daughter, a woman of twenty-six who since she was twelve had suffered from severe tuberculosis and had been unable to talk. Both were cured on the spot. The boy walked home. The woman spoke and no longer had tuberculosis.

Elsewhere in Montichiari was a woman of about thirty-six who had not been normal from birth. Although she "was not completely mentally disturbed," she could not speak and had no control over her bodily functions. At the time of the fourth or fifth apparition, her father went to the cathedral (not the parish church) to supplicate the Lady: "Our dear Lady, if you are really present in the church of Montichiari, please heal our poor sick girl." At the same moment back home, the incontinent woman was completely healed.

The miracle cures caused a sensation, but the bishop of the diocese of Brescia, Giacinto Tredici, ordered Pierina to cease her seeing and to work in a convent in Brescia. Pierina obediently went there and for the next nineteen years worked at menial duties. And so it seemed that the apparitions had come to an end by order of the bishop.

In February 1966, however, Pierina was praying in her room when the Lady again appeared to her, saying that she would come again at Fontanelle on the following Easter Sunday, April 17, 1966. When the bishop was told of this, he forbid Pierina to tell anyone about it or go to Fontanelle.

Nonetheless on Easter Pierina went with a friend to Fontanelle and ended up at an old well with a stone staircase leading down to it. It was at the well that the Lady again appeared after the Angelus at noon.

"My Son is all love," said the Lady, "and He sent me here to bestow upon this well healing power. As a sign of penitence and purification, kneel and kiss this top step!" Pierina did so.

"Go further downstairs, stay on your knees and kiss the step again!" Pierina did so.

"Now kiss the steps again and put here a crucifix!" With her left hand the Lady marked the place where the crucifix should be installed. Now the Lady continued:

> *The sick people and all my children shall first ask my Son to forgive them, then they should lovingly kiss this cross, and then they should draw water or drink. Take mud, dirt in your hands, then wash with the water! This is to show that sin becomes mud and dirt in the hearts of my children, but cleansed in the water of grace, souls become clean again and worthy of grace.*
>
> *I wish the sick and all my children to come to this well. Your mission is now here amidst the sick and all who need your help.*

With these words, the Lady rose into the air. She opened her arms and her cloak, "which filled an immense space in the universe." From her arm hung a white rosary.

Below on the right side of her cloak one could see the church of Montichiari where the apparitions and cures had occurred in 1947. Also on the right side of the cloak, one could see the Castle of St. Mary, a fortress built during the Middle Ages on a hill near Montichiari.

Apparently in spite of the bishop's warnings, the news of this apparition had soon spread about — with the result that the well was attended by masses of people wishing to be cured. Very many miraculous cures soon occurred, while those not cured had to live with the apparent fact that their penitence and purification were not sufficient. The sensation caused by the cures was enormous, and the apparitions of the Holy Mother to Pierina Gilli were at least unofficially accepted as those of Our Lady of the Rosa Mystica.

The Castle of St. Mary was for sale at the time, and someone had plans to transform it into an "evil nightclub." Those plans were thwarted, however, when Monsignor Luigi Novarese purchased the castle and converted it into a hospital with an attached house-chapel for old and sick priests. For the solemn inauguration, the parish priest of Montichiari, Monsignor Rossi, invited, among other dignitaries, the bishop of Fátima, João Pereira Vencancio. Thus the apparitions at Montichiari were in very good company.

Now that Pierina Gilli had ecclesiastical permission to receive the apparitions of the Holy Mother, these took place at intervals at least through 1976. The appearances occurred wherever Pierina happened to be. There were at least thirty-six, and there may have been many more.

Later, on April 20, 1969, Pierina Gilli wrote in a letter: "Our Lady has promised to give a sign in the sky to accelerate her triumph." The place where the "sign" was to be manifest was the parish church in Fontanelle.

On the appointed day many people had arrived there early to pray, and hundreds more were on their way. The weather was stormy, the sky covered with gray clouds, the air cold. Suddenly "a space appeared in the clouds." The space swiftly grew darker, until "the sky looked as if night had fallen." People looked at their watches. It was only four in the afternoon.

In the darkening sky, stars could already be seen. The stars continued appearing across the sky until a large crown of twelve stars was visible. In the distance a disc now became visible and grew in size. As it got bigger, it descended toward the people watching. Then it became red with many beautiful shades. It seemed to shake, as if storm-tossed. It arrived at the edge of some clouds and then seemed to fall down.

Everyone was frightened. Many throughout Fontanelle fell down on their knees to pray. The orb stopped its fall, and began "turning on its axis, like a wheel of fire throwing huge flames of fire to the earth." The entire sky over Fontanelle now was lit up with reds. "The sight was described as frightening and incomprehensible."

Suddenly the sun returned into the dark space from out of which it had come. The clouds turned snow white. The usual sun was now seen, radiant white, but still in the dark space. However, this "usual sun" now came out of the dark space in the clouds, moving slowly. It remained still for some moments in the crown of the twelve stars which were still visible. Then, suddenly, it split apart, forming a magnificent cross of light.

By this time, the entire sky had turned yellow, and the clouds seemed to be of sulphur. Again the sun came out of its "dark corridor," like a comet, this time glowing yellow. It shook or danced to and fro. It wandered along the edges of the clouds, rotating again, a large wheel of radiant yellow fire. This spectacle was repeated again and again, something like what had happened at Fátima in 1917.

After some time, the dark space became light again. The stars paled. Clouds again covered the entire sky. For a long time, though, a yellow spot remained — which could be seen from the town of Lonato, about eight miles from Montichiari. The inhabitants of Montichiari and Fontanelle were in an uproar.

Again, on December 8, 1969, extraordinary celestial phenomena were witnessed by vast numbers of people. At about half past two in the afternoon, when the sky was blue, the sun shining warm, suddenly the sun became pink, then soft-glowing white. Everyone could look straight at it "without sunglasses."

Three rays of light were seen emerging from both sides of the sun. It then began to rotate slowly. It changed colors — red to yellow to white, and then back again. Then pink once more. In the middle of the pink, a small blue spot formed. It became larger and rotated as well. It emitted "numerous blue shafts."

The blue shafts had "blue balls" at their ends. They sailed around in the sky. Suddenly they drew together into a geometric design. The design formed itself into what looked like a rosary. The lights of blue descending over all who were watching made the snow on the ground also turn blue. These phenomena lasted for quite some time. All over town, "people watched each other turn colors as they were bathed by the changing rainbow illuminations."

As of December 8, 1969, the apparitions at San Damiano were still ongoing. The stunning apparitions at Zeitoun, Egypt, had commenced in April of 1968 and continued into 1970. And in June 1970 there also occurred the first of the major apparitions at Bayside, Queens, in New York.

19

Zeitoun, Egypt

(1968)

In 1958 Egypt united with Syria to form the United Arab Republic, although the Syrian revolt in 1961 soon led to its dissolution. Even so, in 1961 Egypt embarked on a program of industrialization, chiefly through Soviet technical and economic aid. Both industry and agriculture were almost completely nationalized by the end of 1962. There was a fear among democratic governments that Egypt might become a Soviet satellite.

President Gamal Abdal Nasser set about to make Egypt the undisputed leader of a united Arab world — attacking, in intense propaganda campaigns, other Arab governments that resisted Egypt's leadership. His most effective rallying cry for Arab unity was his denunciations of Israel calling for its total extinction. This rallying cry dominated Middle East politics between 1962 and 1967.

Meanwhile, Egyptian military might continued to increase with the acquisition of powerful modern weapons, many supplied by the USSR. Various militant eruptions ensued, with worldwide impact. In 1967, Nasser assumed near absolute powers by taking over the premiership of the Arab Socialist Union, as Egypt was then called.

International fears increased that Egypt might become fully aligned with the dreaded Soviet Union. Indeed, after the sad war with Israel of 1967, Nasser received a massive infusion of military and economic aid from the Soviet Union. The Western superpowers were quite worried. Such was the state of affairs in 1968.

Zeitoun is a suburb of Cairo. Although the population of Cairo is Moslem, there is also a large Coptic minority in the city, as there is throughout Egypt. In ancient times, the city which became modern Cairo was known as On, or Heliopolis, the latter term Greek for "the City of the Sun." The area of Heliopolis then became known as Mataria, which became the modern town of Zeitoun.

According to Christian tradition, Mataria was the place in Egypt to which the Holy Family fled to escape Herod's attempts to kill the newborn Messiah (Matt. 2:13–18). There once had been a shrine known as St. Mary's Church — built, and several times rebuilt, on the spot the Holy Family had found shelter. At some point the shrine to the Holy Mother disappeared altogether.

In 1925 a member of the Khalil family experienced a "revelation" that the Mother of God would for one year appear in the church to be built there, at the same site. The family donated the land and built the new Coptic St. Mary's Church. But nothing more happened until about forty-six years later, surely when few remembered why the church was built in the first place.

On April 2, 1968, two car mechanics were working in a city garage at Tomanbey Street and Khalil Lane across from the church. One of them happened to glance at the church and was startled to see a "nun" dressed in white standing on top of the dome. He and his colleague thought the nun was going to jump. One ran to get the priest, the other to get the police and an emergency squad.

A large crowd gathered to watch these events — and began commenting on the nun's translucent white radiance. The emergency squad arrived. The crowd increased, and many watched and shouted at the nun not to jump but to come down safely.

But by then the nun began to disappear, and ultimately vanished before everyone's eyes.

The figure atop the church was by many accepted as an appearance of the Blessed Virgin Mary. The appearance caused a small ripple, but life soon went on as usual.

Seven days later, though, the figure was again seen atop the Church of St. Mary's. The luminous figure continued to appear at intervals until some time in 1970 — usually to the awed excitement of as many as 250,000 who gathered to witness her.

Many came armed with cameras. Startling images of the apparition and other phenomena were caught by many, but nothing unusual appeared on other photographs.

It soon became apparent that some could see only indistinct luminosities, and that some saw nothing at all. But the vast majority could see very well. The figure took to walking, or floating, around the dome, descending often to the roof's edges. As she disappeared from one side and appeared on another, loud shouts of joy and awe arose from the masses on the side from which she could be seen.

It wasn't long before the crowds of pilgrims and witnesses achieved massive proportions. The human and motor traffic was tremendous. Shortly after the apparitions commenced, the garage across the street and other nearby buildings were demolished to make room for parking lots to accommodate the visitors.

Father Jerome Palmer, an American priest who witnessed the apparition many times, recorded that it was usually heralded by mysterious lights, bursts so brilliant, flashing, and scintillating that he compared them to sheet lightning. These phenomena preceded the appearance by approximately a quarter of an hour, sometimes appearing above the church and sometimes in "clouds" that formed to cover it like a canopy. The clouds were especially awesome, since clouds are seldom seen in Cairo.

On one occasion, streams of incense poured through the church and settled over the throngs standing outside of it. The fragrance was extraordinary. Often luminous dovelike or birdlike forms glided through the air and sky around the apparition. Their wings did not move. They appeared and disappeared in an instant.

The Lady herself did not stand motionless. In addition to walking around the top of the church, she often bowed and greeted the throngs below. She bent from the waist and moved her arms in greetings and benedictions and blessings. Thousands of people simultaneously knelt to receive them.

The duration of the apparitions varied from a few minutes to sometimes over four hours. On the night of June 8, 1968, the Lady remained visible from 9:00 p.m. until 4:30 a.m. The apparitions continued at intervals through 1970. This was a nonspeaking apparition, but one of glorious magnitude.

Many photos were taken. Among those I've seen, in one the Holy Mother is floating near one of the church's cupolas, suspended in air. No facial features are visible, but the head is clearly surrounded by a nimbus or luminous radiation. The arms and hands are clearly visible. She is sheathed in luminous white light, presumably a gown.

In another photo, a glowing white "bird" appears above her nimbus. In other photos, her head is bowed forward, her hands before her together as if in prayer.

In yet other photos, the dome, cupolas, and outline of the church are suffused with auras, especially the crosses atop the building. There is no other color perceptible but the light, which was described by everyone as either whitish-blue or bluish-white.

Sometimes the auras descended to incorporate the hundreds of witnesses close to the church's walls. These were considered fortunately blessed, and so a crowd was always pressed up against the church walls.

The Coptic religious weekly *Watani* was the first to publish information about the apparitions in a spread of two pages each week. The paper also printed weekly accounts of some of the outstanding cures and miracles which took place among the pilgrims and witnesses. Within a short time, media worldwide, including the *New York Times* and major news magazines, were carrying news of the apparition and many photos of it. People from all over the world arrived in increasing numbers — and most of them saw. Sometimes the crowds numbered 250,000 people a night.

With this exquisite apparition, repeated many times, the skeptics' demand of an incontestable photograph of an apparition of the Holy Mother was met, and met many times over. If incontestable photos are accepted as evidence of facts, then the photos of the repeated appearances of the Holy Mother at Zeitoun must be accepted as recording a factual apparition. And, indeed, those photos permit a positive reassessment of all the earlier major apparitions of the Holy Mother.

However, skeptics at Zeitoun wouldn't give up easily. Some of them held that the "Russians are doing it [projecting the image] by means of Telstar." But even if such projection was possible via a space satellite, why the anti-religious Communist Russians would wish to reinforce and support religious faith would have been something of a mystery. But this kind of bewildering "logic" has always been characteristic of skeptical attitudes toward the great apparitions.

The impact of this series of apparitions was tremendous. As stated by Bishop Samuel (then Coptic Bishop of Public, Ecumenical and Social Services):

> *The apparition was for all mankind, since belief in spiritual powers these days is weak. God is trying by all means to help mankind to build up its faith again. We [the Coptic churches] are happy, not only because of the apparitions, but also because of the great phenomena which accompanied them — of cures, of strengthening the faith, of prayerful living.*

The Copts moved expeditiously to "investigate" the apparitions, which, it would seem, hardly needed investigating. On April 23, 1968, only twenty-one days after the apparitions had started, His Holiness Anba Kyrillos VI, Patriarch of the See of

St. Mark in Africa and the Near East, formed a provisional delegation for verifying the matter.

The report of the delegation was very soon published. The report began with an account of the apparitions and expressed deep faith in their validity. "These appearances have been accompanied by two great blessings: the first being that of engendering and strengthening faith, and the second is the miraculous cures of desperate cases."

Some of the medically confirmed cures included those of urinary bladder cancer, cancer of the thyroid gland, permanent blindness, deafness, permanent paralysis of limbs, hernias, high blood pressure, bacteriological and viral infections, and mental derangement.

This was one of the most spectacular events in modern Egyptian history, but it is largely forgotten today.

In any event, Gamal Abdal Nasser suddenly died in 1970. Vice President Anwar al-Sadat succeeded him as president. Sadat followed a modified version of Nasser's hard line toward Israel, but commenced work toward peace accords which has been in process ever since, although another war broke out in 1973.

In July 1972, however, Sadat suddenly ousted all Soviet military personnel stationed in Egypt and placed Soviet bases and equipment under Egyptian control. This represented a reversal of a twenty-year trend of increasing dependence on the USSR — a reversal which caused the Western superpowers immeasurable relief and which may actually have marked the beginning of the end of the Cold War. Whether the gorgeous appearances atop the Church of St. Mary's had anything to do with this — well, no one so far has attempted such an analysis.

20

Bayside, Queens, New York
(1970)

New Yorkers were bemused to learn that an apparition of the Blessed Virgin had been occurring in, of all places, the borough of Queens, just across the East River from Manhattan, in the town of Bayside. The sources of this information were impressive: the venerable *New York Times, Time,* and *Newsweek* all published extensive articles.

If the magnificent apparition at Zeitoun, ending in 1970, had been a nonspeaking one, the one at Bayside, beginning in 1970, was to be exceedingly verbose.

The seer, Veronica Leuken, was born on July 12, 1932, in Flushing, New York. Until the apparitions began she had been a "typical housewife" and mother of five children — one of whom, a son, also had seen the first of the apparitions but was later tragically killed in an accident. Her husband, Arthur, was employed at a local construction company.

Phenomena leading up to the first appearance had begun in 1968 at the time of the assassination of Robert F. Kennedy in Los Angeles. Before it was certain that the Senator was dead, a radio appeal had gone out asking for prayer. Veronica heard this appeal in the car while she was driving her husband to work. She started weeping and framed her prayer in her mind while still driving. At this time she experienced an inexplicable "perfume of roses." A short time later, at home, a small image of St. Theresa, the Little Flower, appeared to her and her son. After this, other phenomena began taking place. At one point she saw a huge cross in the sky which, as she wondered about it, dissolved into an image of the thorn-crowned head of Christ.

The first of many subsequent apparitions of the Holy Mother occurred on June 18, 1970 — which was also the ninth anniversary of the beginning of the apparitions to the young seers at Garabandal, Spain.

The apparition took place outdoors, in front of a statue of Our Lady which stood adjacent to a flagpole in front of the old Church of St. Robert Bellarmine in Bayside Hills in Queens. The Lady announced that she wanted a shrine established on that spot dedicated to "Our Lady of the Roses, Mary Help of Mothers."

Word of this appearance quickly spread. Large crowds began congregating and vigils commenced. Thousands of followers arrived to pray with the entranced seer — while residents had begun protesting the invasion of what had once been a quiet neighborhood.

By 1974, Veronica was conducting prayer services eighty times a year, every Sunday and on every day of religious observation. Pilgrims traveled to Bayside by bus from as far away as Canada. Residents had begun to complain in earnest. The streets were clogged by cars and busses. A potential hazard for emergency vehicles arose. Some residents argued that shrubbery had become a bathroom for Leuken's followers.

The continuing apparitions were also a "source of alarm and antagonism" to the officials of St. Bellarmine's, which had never before been attended in such numbers. The vigils were discouraged by the church and other officials. In November 1973, the statue of Our Lady was removed by orders of the chancellor of the Brooklyn diocese. But the vigils continued nonetheless, and the size of the crowds increased.

By May 1975, local homeowners had organized against the apparitions. The neighbors began marching around the kneeling pilgrims, carrying placards which read "Get out!" and "Leave us alone." Veronica, her now sizeable group of followers, and squads of the pilgrims pleaded freedom of worship. Church officials in Queens and Brooklyn were by now quite frazzled, and some feared that St. Bellarmine's Church, or something else, might catch fire from all the candles.

The events escalated until riot squads of the 111th Precinct of the New York Metropolitan Police had to surround the area to protect the pilgrims — an action that further infuriated the neighbors and resulted in greater press coverage, which enlarged the already large number of pilgrims.

A court case ensued, accompanied by extensive media coverage. Monsignor J. Emmett McDonald, former pastor of St. Robert Bellarmine Church, had refused repeatedly to accept the possibility that the Bayside apparitions might be authentic. The monsignor even had appeared on TV to indicate that the apparitions and its messages were "the product of a fertile imagination." But thousands of pilgrims thought they were not, and the situation became increasingly tense and threatening.

The court case was a drawn-out and complicated one during which support for Veronica increased. The situation was not helped when Monsignor McDonald and the chancellor of the Brooklyn diocese, Monsignor James P. King, joined together on the media program *The First Estate — Religion in Review* to discredit Veronica and the apparitions and to discourage the pilgrims.

As the situation and the court case increased in complexity, the Lady indicated to Veronica in one of her kneeling trances that "the offer of the chief of police" was to be accepted. It indeed turned out that the chief of police had feverishly been searching for a solution before riots took place. After consultation with authorities, he offered Veronica the site of the Vatican Pavilion at the old World's Fair Grounds in Flushing Meadows Park near Shea Stadium.

That immense location had been standing empty since 1964.

It was large enough to hold the pilgrims, who now numbered six to ten thousand strong. There was enough space to accommodate processions three miles long. Veronica accepted the offer, the court case was resolved, and only minimal numbers of police needed to be assigned when vigils were held. Although the secular side of the problem was now organized, church authorities avoided the apparition and its implications. The Bayside appearances were an affair of the grassroots devout.

For many years this devotion was enormous. When I first visited one of the vigils in the summer of 1976, I was flabbergasted to count no less than 118 chartered busses parked near the pavilion site, more than half of which were double-deckers. They had arrived from Missouri, Wisconsin, Nevada, Tennessee. The throngs of pilgrims were so huge that for some time I could not locate the center of the events or where the procession of thousands was taking place.

Sometime before 1972, Our Lady of the Roses indicated a tangible proof of the authenticity of her presence was needed "to communicate with a fallen generation, a generation whose hearts are so hardened, whose minds are so closed, and whose eyes are so blinded."

As the Lady instructed, the tangible proof was to be in the form of Polaroid photographs. Pilgrims were to attend the vigils with self-developing Polaroid cameras and snap away at anything they wanted. Upon some of the photos would appear the "tangible proof." Since Polaroid film develops within a few seconds after it is ejected from the camera, this would eliminate accusations of tampering with negatives.

Among the thousands of pilgrims countless flash bulbs went off, and the soft whirring and buzzing of thousands of Polaroid cameras producing developed photographs could be heard. Some didn't use flashbulbs and simply photographed the darkness after night had fallen at the site.

The "miraculous photos" obtained this way were not very many compared to the size of the crowds, but did number in the hundreds. And those colored photos were astonishing, especially after numerous film experts could not explain them at all, nor could Polaroid Company experts. Indeed, direct photographic evidence of the presence of the Holy Mother was acquired by a Polaroid camera. One of the self-developing photos quite clearly showed her image above the old St. Robert Bellarmine Church.

Thereafter, numerous photos of Veronica during vigils revealed beams of light shining down on her from some source above and out of the pictures' frames. In fact, all kinds of beautiful and wonderful lights, images, saints, colors, faces, mists, bubbles, and streams appeared on the photos.

On November 1, 1975, a lady from Massachusetts who had undergone two unsuccessful back operations and come to the vigil on crutches was instantaneously cured. As she dropped her crutches and walked alone and upright, many cameras snapped away. In one of the photos could be seen a glowing white shape taken to be that of the Lady — with transparent images of the now unneeded crutches behind her.

Many of the miraculous photos seemed to illustrate the content of the messages being given at the time they were taken. The organization that had grown around Veronica issued a pamphlet which decoded the colors, numbers, shapes, and symbols which appeared in the miraculous photos. For example, blue denoted the presence of Our Lady; pink, that of Our Lord; green, that of the holy Archangel St. Michael. Mauve or purple denoted suffering or sorrow.

When I visited the vigils, I went armed with my Polaroid and several packs of film, all to no avail. But I saw with my own eyes several miraculous photos appear. In one case, after I had run out of film, I started talking with three women from Canada who had plenty of extra film, but wouldn't sell me any.

One of these women was snapping away without focusing on anything in particular. Nothing unusual was appearing on the photos. But then there appeared a photo that slowly turned into a field of exquisite dark blue laced with electricity-like "strands" of white light. Among the strands were tiny, but very recognizable faces of *angels and their wings*.

At this, the three Canadian women burst into tears, and I did too. I immediately offered $200 for the photo. At this moment, though, a tremendous cheer went up among those now gathered in awe, and the crying woman was bustled away among them. I later saw the photo attached to a large statue of the Virgin Mary being carried on men's shoulders in the procession.

The photos indeed can be considered miraculous and supernatural. But the messages of Our Lady of the Roses also have to be considered — and there were many of them though the years. Veronica was supplied with a tape recorder, and when she fell into her trances she described what she was seeing and then repeated the messages, which were recorded. A written rendition was then quickly provided, printed, and distributed. Two oversized volumes together comprising 1,004 pages were eventually published, containing the messages conveyed between 1970 and 1984.

Almost from the start of the apparitions, Our Lady of the Roses sternly commented upon such delicate matters as corruption within the Catholic Church, with special attention to the "evil" in the Vatican itself and among the clergy. Our Lady of the Roses referred to New York City as "that cesspool of perversion." She warned of the increase of aberrant sex and use of drugs. She warned about the "creation of a youth without morals" through the implementation of the long-term psychopolitical "brainwashing" techniques of education and television. All of this, she said, was preparatory to "the raising of a mindless generation of young adults who will accept without resistance the birthing plans of world hegemony."

She warned of the adverse results of "rock-music business under the control of an international group who worship the Devil." The Lady tackled the intrigues of the Illuminati whose "hegemony" was antireligious, anti-individualistic, opposed to "freedom of the masses," and "infused with control" both mental and physical. She continuously warned of the coming "world government and one-world Satanic religion."

Flying saucers were "the demonic agents of hell traveling in transports." Society was "riddled with false miracles" of the times and lusts for more of them. The manipulators hidden behind the structures of "money, media, and economy" came under continuous attack, while the "Russian Bear" — the Soviet Union and international Communism — was vividly denounced.

Our Lady of the Roses predicted that the "killing of sixteen million American babies in the womb" would take place because of rampant lack of judgment, morals, and individual responsibility. Droughts, famines, rotting crops, hurricanes, and earth tremors will increase "in proportion to the worse and more evil man allows himself to become." There will be an onslaught of mysterious diseases, and a new war will cause the destruction of cities.

The Lady indicated that sooner or later individual and collective "sin brings the chastisement of God." After the world has suffered an apocalypse of its own making, God will send "a Ball of Redemption" to wipe out most of what is left. And indeed, large red balls of light appeared in many of the miraculous photos, often amid mauve (=suffering) and purple (=sorrow) lights and mists.

All of this — unless people worked and prayed for peace.

Much more along these lines was included in the ongoing messages. The seer herself didn't understand many of the messages and had to ask others to explain them. This was taken as evidence that she couldn't have invented what she didn't understand in the first place.

Beginning early in the apparitions, the Holy Mother had constantly pleaded for prayer for Pope Paul VI, indicating that he was suffering much. Then, on September 27, 1975, and to the astonishment of all, the Lady indicated that ruling in the pope's place was "an *imposter* created from the minds of the agents of Satan.... The best of [plastic] surgeons were used to create this *imposter*. Shout it from the rooftops!"

The meaning was that Pope Paul VI had become incapacitated or had died and had been replaced by an imposter. As outrageous

as this might seem, independent suspicions along these lines soon
surfaced in Europe when it was noticed that Pope Paul's face,
nose, and ears had changed shape.

Comparative voice analysis of the pope on Easter, 1975, and
"the pope" on Christmas, 1975, showed inconsistencies. There
was a huge flap in Europe over this, summarized in 1977 in
a book by Theodore Kolberg entitled *The Deception of the
Century,* which included comparative photographic evidence.

Our Lady of the Roses later advised that the successor to the
imposter Paul VI, Pope John Paul I, had reigned for only thirty-
three days because he had been "murdered by poisoning." And
the Lady named names. Indeed, independently of the Bayside
messages, the sudden death of the new pope inspired conspiracy
theories along the same lines.

Our Lady of the Roses never minced words — but such words
forever closed the minds of religious authorities against this
apparition.

During the mid-1980s, the seer became ill, and I was told that
Our Lady of the Roses rarely appeared to her. Then on October 6, 1985, my phone rang. A devout friend of the Lady
breathlessly told me that she had predicted in her message of
October 5, 1985, that there would soon be an earthquake in
New York City, where earthquakes are exceedingly rare. This
prediction was in print and circulation by the end of that week.
Two quakes rocked New York City on October 19 and 21. The
epicenter was fifteen miles north of mid-town Manhattan.

21

Medjugorje, Yugoslavia
(1981)

The complicated political entity on the Balkan Peninsula known as Yugoslavia was created as a result of World War I. It was composed of six republics. The ethnic groups of the republics are closely related linguistically. But historical, ethnic, and religious factors have kept them separate until today. The Croats and Slovenes, about 30 percent of the population, are Roman Catholic; about 40 percent of the Yugoslavs adhere to the Orthodox Eastern Church; and about 10 percent belong to Islam. The majority of the Muslims live in Bosnia and Hercegovina. This combined political entity is slightly smaller than the state of Nevada, with a population, in 1981, of about twenty million.

The move to unification in 1914 was a major cause of World War I. The unification was roughly achieved after the war as the "Kingdom of the Serbs, Croats, and Slovenes." This name was changed only in 1921 to "Yugoslavia." In 1929 King Alexander established a royal dictatorship in order to contain the combative ethnic groupings. King Alexander was later assassinated, and the Communist party gained in strength.

The Soviet army entered Belgrade in 1944, and by 1945 the non-Communist members of the government had been arrested. Yugoslavia then became an extension of the Soviet Empire. The Communist government stabilized the nation by totalitarian controls — and so the world in general gladly forgot the traditional ethnic-religious ferments which continued simmering beneath those controls. The Communists suppressed and persecuted all religious expressions, religion being the "enemy" in Communist philosophy. So Yugoslavia seemed a very unlikely place for the occurrence of a great apparition of the Holy Mother.

On June 24, 1981, at about 6:15 p.m., two young girls were walking on the hill of Podbrdo on Mount Krisevach in the parish of Medjugorje. On a barren rock path they encountered a luminous silhouette of a woman hovering about three feet above the ground. She was dressed in gray garments and wearing a white veil. Her face, though, was "shining brightly." It was the feast day of John the Baptist.

Ivanka Ivankovich, age fifteen, thought it was the Virgin Mary, but her companion, Mirjana Dragicevich, age sixteen, said "No, it couldn't be the Virgin Mary." Both were afraid, and hastily returned to town, where they collected two other young people, Vicka Ivankovich, seventeen, and Ivan Dragicevich, sixteen.

The four now returned to the place on hill. All four saw the Lady. But none dared to say anything to her. The group then rushed back to their hamlet, Bijakovici in the Medjugorje parish, and began telling what they had seen. Nobody believed them and they were teased. Some suggested they had seen a flying saucer. Vicka's grandmother suggested throwing holy water on the figure if it appeared again because "the devil can't stand holy water."

But by the next day, Thursday, June 25, everyone in the hamlet was talking about the event. After school and chores, two of the youths (some versions say all four) set off for the hill. Along the way they picked up Marija Pavlovich, sixteen, who was babysitting Jakov Colo, who was ten. Two adults accompanied the group of young people. They found the Lady waiting for them. Some sources say that Vicka tossed holy water on her, and she smiled. The youngest youth, Jakov Colo, fell to his knees, the rest followed, and they all began praying the rosary. The two adults saw nothing, but knelt and prayed anyway.

People in the surrounding villages of Bijakovici, Medjugorje,

Miletina and others as far away as Citluk, soon heard of the apparition, which was now understood to be that of the Blessed Virgin Mary. On Friday, June 26, in the late afternoon, a crowd of two to three thousand had gathered. The press of people was so great that Mirjana and Ivanka fainted. A neighbor, Marinko Ivankovich, from then on became their protector guarding them from the crowds.

Almost everyone gathered now saw the miraculous lights at the Podbrdo (which means "foot of the hill"). The children raced up the barren and rocky hill, while the gathered crowd quickly scrambled up after them. The children went to a place about 150 feet higher than the spot where the first two apparitions had taken place. There they knelt and may have entered into a trance. They began singing and then began reciting the rosary, as most of the large group on the hill also did. They also recited, for the first time, the traditional prayer of the area: seven times the Our Father, Hail Mary, and Glory Be to the Father, to which the Lady had them add the Creed. They also had conversations with the Lady and asked: "Who are you?" The reply was unambiguous: "I am the Blessed Virgin Mary." The appearance came to an end between 7:00 and 7:30 p.m.

When questioned about what the Lady had said, all the seers repeated in unison: "Peace! Peace! Peace! Be reconciled!" All the seers, whether together or separately, would report future messages with the same exact words.

There is some confusion in the sources regarding the identity of the first seers. They were now to be Vicka, Mirjana, Ivanka, Marija, Ivan, and Jakov. A sister of Marija, Milka, who apparently had seen the first apparition, did not see it the third time nor thereafter.

On the morning of the fourth day, Saturday, June 27, the six young seers were summoned to Citluk to be interrogated by the police. They were questioned "at length and harshly," but they remained firm and unshaken. They were then required to undergo psychiatric examinations by Dr. Ante Vujevich, who found them "normal, balanced, and in good health."

That evening the apparition took place again, and again the next day, Sunday, June 28. By this time the crowds had grown to some fifteen thousand. Miracle cures took place. A blind man recovered his sight, and a paralyzed child carried up the hill walked back down. Hundreds of conversions took place, and the converts went to local churches to confirm them, much to the astonishment and consternation of the few clergy. And the greatest miracle of all occurred: a great religious awakening of the region around Medjugorje had begun — which was soon to electrify the world.

The Communists, however, were not at all pleased with these developments. Only six days into the apparitional sequence, all of the young seers were promptly summoned by officials to the city of Mostar. There the officials at first held that the youths should be committed to a psychiatric ward — which was not unusual in a Communist state which did not hesitate to confine dissidents, fanatics, and the politically incorrect.

Upward of fifteen thousand people attending upon a proclaimed apparition of the Holy Mother must have been a matter of grave concern for the Communist authorities. But the matter was also delicate, because such an enormous crowd could riot if their religious and devotional fervor was interfered with. Thus, after a medical examination by a Dr. Dzuda, who "confirmed their perfect psychological balance," the seers were promptly returned to their village the same day.

That evening, with an even larger crowd in attendance, the Holy Mother proclaimed, "There is but one God, one faith, believe strongly, have confidence."

The seers also asked that a mute and paralyzed youth be healed, one "little Danijel," whose parents were quite sad about his condition. "Let them believe firmly, and he will be healed," said the Holy Mother. The child was cured.

The next day all six seers were whisked away on a long day trip by two women who came for that purpose. The trip was scheduled to last beyond the usual time of the apparition and clearly was arranged by local authorities to thwart the appearance. At the usual time of the apparition, however, when the car was slowly heading back toward Medjugorje, the seers asked that the car be stopped along the road near Cerno. Their tour guides at first refused, but then gave in. At this place, the Lady again appeared to the seers.

Subsequently, the Podbrdo was no longer to be used, and after the issue was discussed with the pastor, Friar Jozo Zovko, the seers began convening in secret in private homes — in accord with official hopes of first discouraging the pilgrims, then the seers.

While reports of the Medjugorje devout avoid much mention of it, the government immediately undertook stronger repressive measures. The six seers were several times taken to police stations and threatened. No automobiles were allowed to enter Medjugorje during the late afternoon or evening. Armed police raided the Franciscan house in the parish and confiscated files and books.

Priests and sisters were arrested, taken to Mostar, and humiliated, but released — except for Father Zovko, who was sentenced for "sedition" to three and a half years in prison. Two priests were arrested for publishing articles on the holy events, and both were sentenced to prison.

The national Communist media viciously attacked the events at Medjugorje, labelling the religious officials linked with the apparition as terrorists of the Nazi-Fascist type. A cartoon of the Blessed Virgin dressed as a terrorist with a knife in her mouth — entitled "The true face of the Blessed Mother" — was published again and again. Ironically, the Communist attacks in the media called national and then world attention to the events at Medjugorje in ways that the Catholic press by itself could never have done.

It was arranged to have Mass celebrated after the apparitions, at the church in Medjugorje, the only place where worship was authorized by the Communist regime. Increasing numbers of pilgrims, alerted by the media blitz, came to the Masses. By January 1982, the seers were permitted to utilize a small room in the church, where they were isolated and out of view of the pilgrims.

It was now far too late to suppress this apparition, and by September 1984, there had been only five days that the Holy Mother did not appear to the six seers. Millions of pilgrims from around the world were making their way to Medjugorje to attend the events there at a rate of about ten thousand a day. I personally have friends who have made the trek to Medjugorje as many as six times. By 1992 fifteen to twenty million people had made their way to the little remote village near the Podbrdo — with impressive economic benefits to the whole region.

International media soon pointed up, somewhat sarcastically, that the government had an embarrassing dilemma between religious suppression and the tourist revenues. Although Yugoslav nationals were discouraged from visiting the site for a while longer, all impediments vanished for international visitors to Medjugorje. The apparitions to the seers have continued on almost a daily basis.

Thousands have claimed to have witnessed miraculous lights and other unusual phenomena. Hundreds, and possibly thousands, have reported cures of disease, physical infirmities, and psychological disorders. There can be no doubt that most of the witnessed phenomena and cures indeed took place.

Many messages have been received, some for the seers themselves and their families, some for priests, bishops, and the pope, and many "secret" ones. Beginning in early 1984, though, the messages received at St. James Parish near Medjugorje were published. Those messages total 224, although the seers experienced many more apparitions than that. One of the threads running throughout the messages, as the seers have all indicated in interviews, is that the appearing Holy Mother at Medjugorje "says a period of darkness has enveloped the planet."

The six seers are now adults. They all insist they are "not important" and are simple and soft-spoken. They all have been subjected to extensive tests regarding their mutual and identical states of ecstasy, which come upon them simultaneously and end simultaneously — much like what happened to the seers at Garabandal. During those states the eyes of each, no matter where they are, turn toward the apparition. Scientists have concluded that "their concurring [identical and simultaneous] body reactions are inexplicable."

One of the Lady's messages at Medjugorje, continuously repeated, was: "Peace! Peace! Peace! Be reconciled!" This plea was not heard very well by the Yugoslavs themselves. Instead, when Communism suddenly collapsed in the Soviet Union in 1989, and shortly after in Yugoslavia, the old ethnic and religious enmities again arose. The response to the Holy Mother's plea for reconciliation was murder, rape, bombing, war — and genocide. Our planet's "period of darkness" had enveloped Yugoslavia.

22

Kibeho, Rwanda
(1981)

The Republic of Rwanda is found in East Central Africa just south of the Equator. The climate is tropical — hot and humid in the lowlands, but cooler in the highlands. The average elevation is about five thousand feet above sea level. Because of its many mountains, ravines, and deep valleys, the country is frequently called "the country of a thousand hills" or the "Switzerland of Africa." Its mountain forests were once abundant and beautiful; most of them have now been stripped away by the needs of human habitation.

In 1978, Rwanda's population was close to five million, and it was the most densely populated nation in Africa. There were three ethnic groups: the Hutus represented 85 percent of the population; the Tutsis were 14 percent; and the Twas about 1 percent. Kinyarwanda and French are the official languages, French reflecting the former Belgian occupation of Rwanda.

In the past, the minority Tutsis (who speak a Nilotic language) had been the traditional overlords of the majority Hutus (who speak Bantu). The descendants of the Hutus have continued to hate the descendants of the Tutsis, a hatred which has periodically flared up into furious violence.

About half of the Rwandans have adhered to their ancient animist beliefs. But most of the other half are Christians, 52 percent of whom are Roman Catholic, with Protestant, Adventist, and Muslim minorities.

Kigali in central Rwanda is the capital and largest city. About thirty miles to the southwest is the second largest town, Butare, see of a Catholic archdiocese. To the west of Butare, is the village of Kibeho, which contains a church and the school buildings of the Rwandan charitable Sisters Benebikira.

On Saturday, November 28, 1981, just after noon, the students in the Kibeho secondary school for young girls were at lunch in the refectory. One of these, Alphonsine Mumureke, age seventeen, had been charged that day with the service. As she would tell later, she was happy, but her joy was mixed with a certain dread. She was anxious because she had several times heard a soft voice which called: "My child, my child."

Apparently the voice had called from a nearby corridor. Alphonsine hesitated for a short while. Then, hearing the voice again, she went into the corridor, knelt, and made the sign of the cross. "I am here," she said. A "Lady of Light" then appeared before her, and a strange conversation took place.

"Lady, who are you?"

"Je suis la Mère du Verbe." (I am the Mother of the Verb.) This opening line of the conversation is difficult largely because no one seems to have really understood what was meant by "Mother of the Verb." In obsolete English, however, "verb" was used to mean "word." "I am the Mother of the Word" might be a correct translation. As it was, this slight confusion was quickly passed over as the Lady asked of Alphonsine: "What do you want [or prefer] of religion?"

Alphonsine responded: "I love God and His Mother, who gave us a Child who saves us!"

"It is thus," spoke the figure, "that I come to reassure you, for I've heard your prayers. I would like your companions to have more faith, because they don't believe sufficiently."

"Mother of the Savior!" responded Alphonsine, who had now recognized the Virgin. "If truly it is you, you who come to say that in our school we have little faith, it is because you love us! I am truly full of joy that you come to me." And with that, the Lady, "full of smiles," vanished by rising upward.

Alphonsine told her lunch companions what she had experienced. Her story was not well received. She was mocked and someone accused her of wanting to make herself special because she was not originally from the Kibeho region and because she was an outsider since she had arrived at the school after it had already started.

Several recurrences of the apparition followed, and Alphonsine apparently had acquired that stubborn quality characteristic of seers, that is, they will not back down or recant. Some of her fellow students had begun kneeling and praying with her, although they couldn't see the apparition. Alphonsine had been challenged to ask the Virgin to manifest herself to others as well. Alphonsine put this request to the Lady. And on January 12, 1982, Anathalie Mukamazimpaka saw Our Lady and fell into the same ecstasy as Alphonsine.

Excitement and consternation invaded the village of Kibeho. At some point, the seers faced vigorous opposition by Marie-Claire Mukangango, a confidante of Monsignor Gahamanyi, bishop of the archdiocese of Butare. The increasingly delicate situation was resolved on March 2, 1982, when Marie-Claire Mukangango found that she too could see the apparition.

In July, a young boy, Segatshaya, not then a Christian, also saw, as did another boy, Valentine, and also four other girls — Agnes, Vestine, Stephanie, and another younger Agnes. There were to be eight principal seers, although about twenty in the Kibeho area claimed to have seen the Lady, and at least ten more in other parts of the country. An apparition of Jesus also occasionally appeared to some of the seers. The Lady had been requested to permit others to see her if she was really the Holy Mother. The Holy Mother apparently had complied. The eight principal seers at Kibeho, though, were the only ones quickly accepted as authentic.

Each of the principal seers were questioned and interrogated both separately and together. Their descriptions of the Lady differed. But whether separately or together, all of them unanimously and passionately agreed about one aspect of the apparition — something which had never occurred in any other apparition, so far as I can determine.

The landscape in the Kibeho and Butare area was one of man-made desolation, for it was almost entirely denuded of all plant life, taken either for firewood or some other practical use. It was a blighted region of rocks and dirt, hot, dry, and dusty between infrequent rains and miserably muddy when rain did fall. Famine was a perpetual threat unless food was transported into the area.

Some of the seers said that the Lady at Kibeho was a beautiful white woman, sometimes, but not always like a European lady. The Lady's appearance was slightly different to different seers, and slightly different at times to the same seers. "It was very difficult to describe the color of her complexion — neither black nor white, nor mulatto very much, but was rather like a color a little gilded, exactly as the complexion of women in the Far East." All were unanimous regarding the Lady's beauty. Some said she was dressed all in white, a robe descending to her feet, with a sparkling veil which covered her entirely. Others said the veil was blue, something like a cape. All agreed that the appearing figure was luminous.

When the seers were overtaken by their intense ecstatic trances, they all lost all contact with "this world." They were "tested" while in these trances. They were picked at by pens and knife points, and sometimes blood flowed. Lit matches and candles were applied to their hands. Flashlights were shined directly into their wide, staring eyes. The pupils neither contracted nor dilated. Some were slapped across the face, without any response. Their bodies were frozen into place; their arms and legs could not be moved by force.

While in these trances with the young, luminous Holy Mother they were in another world, a vast expanse of vivid green meadows laden with glittering moisture and dew. The sky above was radiant with soft pink and other colored lights. And there were flowers everywhere, radiant and glowing. In this landscape, so different from that at Kibeho, the Virgin Mary floated above the seers — which is why they all had their heads bent back and looked almost directly upward. This same wondrous landscape was identically described by all the seers.

The first apparitions had taken place in the dormitory of the school. To accommodate everyone who wanted to watch, the original box-like dormitory space was soon converted into a larger chapel by removing the partitions.

Soon, though, many of the pilgrims couldn't fit into the contrived chapel and began demanding that the seers receive Our Lady outside. So the apparitions began taking place in front of the dormitory in the courtyard of the school. But more and more pilgrims arrived, and the seers were hard to view even in the enclosed courtyard.

One Brother Graton, of the Pères Blancs Missionaries, had the idea of erecting an elevated podium not far from the school. This was surrounded by fences to keep back the immense and growing crowd of pilgrims and was built "as high as a man." Atop this platform where everyone could view them even from afar, the young seers singly or together assumed their trances, and again their necks arched backward.

The Lady always announced her next apparition, and on those dates the masses of pilgrims increased. So that "all could listen and profit from the dialogues from heaven" the seers repeated the Lady's words as they took place. They were equipped with microphones and the surrounding area "was provided with many sound boxes." Later Radio Rwandaise installed a more effective loud-speaker system and began live broadcasting of descriptions of the events and the messages.

The main theme of the messages was that people do not pay sufficient attention to the things of heaven. The truths revealed in the Bible are considered out of date or irrelevant, and people ignore them. "For example," the Lady pointed out, "the end times predicted in the Bible leave them indifferent, and they don't prepare themselves or see the necessity to aim for perfection."

"Everything I tell them," the Lady complained, "seems unimportant to them." This complaint is, of course, an echo of other apparitions, especially the one at Kerizinen, France, beginning in 1938. But this apparition was not accepted by the church and had become quite obscure by 1981. It is unlikely that the young seers at Kibeho had ever heard of Kerizinen.

Many pilgrims, police, and government officials were on hand to witness the remarkable solar phenomena which sometimes occurred. The witnesses included many priests and nuns, most of whom gave written testaments. One of these, written by a Rwandan priest, concluded that "the priests of the Grand Seminary who are part of the Theological Commission...have objectively witnessed these phenomena."

One could stare at the sun without damage to the eyes. It first became blue-tinted. Then the upper part appeared white and brilliant, while the lower part was red. There was something "like a headband" running through the middle of the sun. The sun began to dance from the left to the right, and down and up, for about ten minutes. And thousands of witnesses saw the sky over Kibeho shifting across a delightful spectrum of tinted colors. At night, sometimes the stars danced and sometimes they disappeared altogether, to be replaced by luminous crosses. And perhaps most important to the drought-stricken Kibeho area, were the rains.

The idea of the rain apparently was the Lady's. "Why have you not asked me for water?" she asked Anathalie in August, a month when it seldom rained.

Anathalie responded: "You have said that you give as you will and when you want."

And the Holy Mother replied: "And now I will give you a rain of consecration."

Shortly thereafter, a thunderstorm broke, and so began the first of many heavy rains. But no one ran for shelter. Instead the thousands of gathered pilgrims knelt in the downpour, knelt in the welcome mud, exalting in the "rains from heaven." The rain water was gathered into every obtainable container and into huge cooking cauldrons. And from these collected waters the cures began.

The ultimate "approval" of Our Lady at Kibeho could not have been in much doubt practically from the first — because of video tapes, radio broadcasts, and priestly witnesses, because of the solar miracles and cures. The responsibility for approval fell to the bishop of the archdiocese of Butare, Monsignor Gahamanyi. This prelate, "based in reason and prudence," was not content to interview the seers alone. He convoked two commissions of study. One was composed of medical doctors and psychiatrists, the other of theologians. The commissions independently tested the seers, conducted interviews, and examined the "facts at Kibeho." But there already had been an "enormous renewal of devotion," an increase of faith, and countless conversions not only at Kibeho, but throughout Rwanda.

Among the many messages given at Kibeho were ominous warnings. These were received either while the seers were in a trance or when they lay in an unexplainable, death-like coma for two or three days and nights. At first those in a coma were thought to be dead, but minimal vital signs were detected by medical doctors. Although harsh measures were undertaken to arouse the comatose seers, nothing did so. Those who experienced the comas experienced "mysterious voyages," "visions of horror," the "sadness of Jesus," and the "end of the world."

On August 15, 1982, after five of the principal seers recovered from their communal ecstasy lasting eight hours, all fell into trembling heaps of tears and terror. All reported having been given a frightful tour of a scene of torrents of blood, bodies abandoned without burial, trees on fire, great abysses opening up, an appalling monster, and decapitated heads everywhere. Some twenty-five hundred pilgrims who were present were themselves very afraid, and these visions of apocalypse were repeated several times. Most surprisingly, the Lady warned most of the seers to leave Rwanda. The social-political events that developed after this wondrous apparition were to be of great horror, and the Lady's awful apocalypse was to be fulfilled.

Four years later, the wars between the Hutus and Tutsis flared out of control. The goal of the Hutus was the complete genocide of the Tutsis. The Hutu leaders ordered all Hutu males, as young as six and as old as ninety, to kill at least one Tutsi — and to cut off and show their heads as proof they had done so. Towns, villages, and hamlets with their trees were burned to the ground. Thousands upon thousands of bodies were abandoned and left unburied. Rivers turned putrid with rotting corpses everywhere. People died of fever if they drank from them. So enormous was the pollution from dead bodies of Hutu and Tutsi alike that fish even died in the great Kivu Lake, some sixty miles long, on the western border of Rwanda.

Hundreds of thousands of refugees fled into neighboring countries. Vast amounts of aid came from other countries and from the United Nations, but the aid was not nearly enough, and thousands more died in refugee camps, especially children who were already suffering from malnutrition in their homeland. Apocalypse had truly descended on Rwanda as the Holy Mother had warned.

No accurate account of the loss to Rwanda's four million population is available as I write in October 1995. But the body count may be as great as one half the population. Apocalypse truly descended on Rwanda as the Holy Mother had warned in her apparitions there.

Epilogue

When the accounts of thousands upon thousands of eyewitness to the holy apparitions are heeded, when the apparitions are considered in their social-political contexts, when the amazing phenomena are fairly presented (the celestial events, the warnings, the fulfilled predictions, the cures, the other astonishing phenomena), when the photographs taken at Zeitoun and San Damiano and Bayside are considered — what are we to think? The part of the apocalypse given at La Salette in 1846 regarding the coming agonizing pollution of "earth's glove" (our atmosphere) is surely remarkable and extraordinary.

If we try to be as practical, as pragmatic as possible, as logical and perhaps even as scientific as possible, what are we to conclude? Surely it must be admitted that something truly remarkable took place at each of the great apparitions considered in this book.

And what of the Holy Mother's signal request, reiterated again and again in all of the great speaking apparitions: "Pray! Pray! Pray! Pray for peace! Be reconciled!" Those who truly do pray for peace, whether Catholic, Protestant, Coptic, or otherwise, are unlikely to be among those who devote themselves to creating violence.

Great apparitions of the Holy Mother have occurred on an average of about every ten years or so during the modern period. The last two of the great apparitions took place during the very early 1980s, those in Yugoslavia and in Rwanda.

So we are slightly overdue for another great one.

Bibliography

Agnellet, Michel. *Miracles à Fátima.* Paris: Editions de Trevise, 1958.

Auclair, Raoul. *Kerizinen: Apparitions en Bretagne?* Paris: Nouvelles Editions Latines, 1968.

Barthas, Chanoine C. *Les apparitions de Fátima.* Paris: Le Livre Chrétien, 1952.

Billet, Bernard, et al. *Vrais et fausses apparitions dans L'Eglise.* Paris: Editions P. Lethielleux, 1971.

Carlier, L. *Histoire de l'apparition de la Mère de Dieu sur le montagne de la Salette.* Tournai: Les Missionnaires de la Salette, 1912.

Carol, Juniper B. *Fundamentals of Mariology.* New York: Benziger Bros., 1956.

Cartwright, John K. *The Catholic Shrines of Europe.* New York: McGraw-Hill, 1955.

Castella, A. *Maria erscheint in San Damiano.* Hauteville, Switzerland: Parvia Verlag, 1985.

Cruz, Joan Carroll. *The Incorruptibles.* Rockford, Ill.: TAN Books and Publishers, 1977.

Gebara, I., and M. Bingemer. *Mary, Mother of God, Mother of the Poor.* Trans. Phillip Berryman. Maryknoll, N.Y.: Orbis Books, 1989.

González, Conchita. *Miracle at Garabandal.* Garden City, N.Y.: Doubleday, 1983.

Delaney, John J. *A Woman Clothed with the Sun.* New York: Doubleday, 1960.

Derobert, Abbé. *Apparitions au Rwanda.* Paris: Editions Jules Hovine, 1984.

Englebert, Omer. *Catherine Labouré and the Modern Apparitions of Our Lady.* New York: P. J. Kennedy & Sons, 1958.

Haffert, John M. *Meet the Witnesses.* Fátima, Portugal: AMI International Press, 1961.

Higgins, Paul Lambourne. *Mother of All.* Minneapolis: T. S. Denison, 1969.

Historiques des apparitions de Tilly-sur-Seulles. 4 vols. Paris: Dentu, 1901.

Jaouen, J. *La grâce de la Salette 1846–1946.* Paris: Cerf, 1946.

Johnston, Francis. *Fátima: The Great Sign.* Rockford, Ill.: TAN Books and Publishers, 1979.

———. *The Wonder of Guadalupe.* Rockford, Ill.: TAN Books and Publishers, 1981.

Kerkhofs, L. *Notre-Dame de Banneux.* Liège: Dessain, 1972.

La Douceur, E. *The Children of La Salette.* New York: Vantage Press, 1965.

Laffineur, M., and M. T. le Pelletier. *Star on the Mountain.* Trans. S. I. Lacouture. Newtonville, N.Y.: Our Lady of Mount Carmel of Garabandal, 1968.

Laurentin, René. *Catherine Labouré*. Paris: Desclée de Brouwer, 1981.

———. *Is the Virgin Mary Appearing at Medjugorje?* Washington, D.C.: The Word Among Us Press, 1984.

Manuel, David. *Medjugorje under Siege*. Orleans, Mass.: Paraclete Press, 1992.

Marnham, Patrick. *Lourdes*. London: Heinemann, 1980.

Massart, Chanoine. *Leçons de Beauraing*. Beauraing, Belgium: Editions Pro Maria, 1951.

Miraculous Lady of the Roses at San Damiano, Italy (written by a devotee of Padre Pio). Hickory Corners, Mich.: Miraculous Lady of the Roses, 1970.

Our Lady of the Roses, Mary Help of Mothers: A Book about the Heavenly Apparitions to Veronica Lueken at Bayside, New York (no author). Lansing, Mich.: Apostles of Our Lady, 1981.

Page Research Library, comp. *Apparition Phenomenon Manifest at Zeitoun, Cairo, Egypt*. Cleveland, 1975.

Palmer, Jerome. *Our Lady Returns to Egypt*. San Bernardino, Calif.: Culligan Publications, 1969.

Pelletier, Joseph A. *The Sun Danced at Fátima*. Garden City, N.Y.: Doubleday, 1983.

Renso, Don. *Our Lady Speaks to Her Beloved Priests*. Milan, Italy: The Marian Movement of Priests, 1983.

Richard, Abbé H. *What Happened at Pontmain?* Washington, N.J.: Ave Maria Institute, 1971.

Saint-Pierre, Michel de. *Bernadette and Lourdes*. Garden City, N.Y.: Doubleday, 1955.

Sánchez-Ventura y Pascual, R. *Garabandal*. Paris: Les Nouvelles Editions Latines, n.d.

Scheetz, Leo A. *Necedah: Believe It or Not*. Necedah, Wis.: For My God And My Country, 1982.

Smith, Jody Brant. *The Image of Guadalupe*. Garden City, N.Y.: Doubleday, 1983.

Swan, Henry H. *My Work with Necedah*. 5 vols. Necedah, Wis.: For My God And My Country, 1959.

Testimonials of Pilgrims at Necedah. 5 vols. Necedah, Wis.: For My God And My Country, n.d.

Thompson, C. J. S. *The Mystery and Lore of Apparitions*. New York: Frederick A. Stokes, 1920.

Thurston, Herbert. *Beauraing and Other Apparitions*. London: Burns Oates & Washbourne, 1934.

———. *The Physical Phenomena of Mysticism*. Chicago: Henry Regnery, 1952.

Villaneuva, Francisco. *Wonders of Lipa*. Manila, Philippines: Grand Avenue Book Store, 1949.

Walsh, Michael. *The Apparition at Knock*. Tuam, Ireland: St. Jarlath's College, 1959.

Walsh, William J. *The Apparitions and Shrines of Heaven's Bright Queen*. 4 vols. London: Burns & Oates, 1904.

Walsh, William Thomas. *Our Lady of Fátima.* Garden City, N.Y.: Doubleday, 1954.

Warner, Marina. *Alone of All Her Sex: The Myth and the Cult of the Virgin Mary.* New York: Random House, 1976.

Weigl, A. M. *Mary — Rosa Mystica — Montichiari-Fontanelle.* Altotting, Germany: St. Grignion-Verlag, 1974.

Zaki, Pearl. *Our Lord's Mother Visits Egypt in 1968 and 1969.* Cairo, Egypt: Patriarch of the See of St. Mark, n.d.